PSHE and citizenship
ages 5–7

Gillian Goddard & Jacqueline Barbera

Published by Scholastic Ltd,
Villiers House,
Clarendon Avenue,
Leamington Spa,
Warwickshire
CV32 5PR
www.scholastic.co.uk

Printed by Ebenezer Baylis & Son Ltd, Worcester
Text © 2002 Gillian Goddard and Jacqueline Barbera
© 2002 Scholastic Ltd
1 2 3 4 5 6 7 8 9 0   2 3 4 5 6 7 8 9 0 1

Authors

Gillian Goddard and Jacqueline Barbera

Editor

Christine Harvey

Assistant Editor

Dulcie Booth

Series designer

Lynne Joesbury

Designer

Mark Udall

Illustrations

Martha Hardy

Cover illustration

Jill Newton

British Library Cataloguing-in-Publication Data
A catalogue record for this book is available from the British Library.

ISBN 0-439-02000-X

Designed using Adobe Pagemaker

Contents

Acknowledgements

Andersen Press Ltd for an extract and illustration from *The Three Pigs* by Tony Ross © 1983, Tony Ross (1983, Andersen Press). **Andersen Press Ltd** for an extract from *Not Now, Bernard* by David McKee © 1980, David McKee (1980, Andersen Press). **Andersen Press Ltd** for an extract and illustration from *Michael* by Tony Bradman and Tony Ross. Text © 1990, Tony Bradman. Illustration © 1990, Tony Ross (1990, Andersen Press). **Andersen Press Ltd** for text from *Elmer* by David McKee © 1989, David McKee (1989, Andersen Press). **Patrick Benson and Walker Books** for an illustration from *Read and Respond: Owl Babies* by Sue Palmer, based on characters from *Owl Babies* by Martin Waddell. Illustration © 2000, Patrick Benson (2000, Scholastic Ltd). **Caroline Binch** for an illustration from *Read and Respond: Amazing Grace* by Judith Graham based on the book *Amazing Grace* by Mary Hoffman © 1997, Caroline Binch (1997, Scholastic Ltd). **Peter Dixon** for the poem 'Infant School Disaster' from *Grow your own poems* by Peter Dixon © 1988, Peter Dixon (1988, Peche Luna). **Egmont Children's Books Ltd** for an extract and illustration from *The Three Little Wolves and the Big Bad Pig* by Eugene Trivizas and Helen Oxenbury. Text © 1993, Eugene Trivizas. Illustration © 1993, Helen Oxenbury (1993, Heinemann). **AM Heath and Co on behalf of Judith Viorst** for an extract from *The tenth good thing about Barney* by Judith Viorst © 1971, Judith Viorst (1971, William Collins Sons and Co Ltd). **David Higham Associates** for 'The Quarrel' by Eleanor Farjeon from *Silver-Sand and Snow* by Eleanor Farjeon © 1951, Eleanor Farjeon (1951, Michael Joseph). **John Johnson (Authors' Agent)** for 'Hair' by Max Fatchen from *Songs for my dog and other wry rhymes* by Max Fatchen © 1980, Max Fatchen (1980, Kestrel). **Frances Lincoln Ltd** for an extract from *Amazing Grace* by Mary Hoffman © 1991, Mary Hoffman (1991, Frances Lincoln Ltd). **Frances Lincoln Ltd** for an extract and one illustration from *MINE!* By Hiawyn Oram and Mary Rees. Text © 1992, Hiawyn Oram. Illustrations © 1992, Mary Rees (1992, Frances Lincoln Ltd). **Little, Brown and Co Inc** for an extract from *Osa's Pride* by Ann Grifalconi © 1990, Ann Grifalconi (1990, Little, Brown and Co Inc). **Amy Makin** for *Getting ready for bed* by Amy Makin © 2002, Amy Makin, previously unpublished. **David McKee** for two illustrations from *Read and Respond: Not Now, Bernard* by Hilary Braund and Deborah Campbell, based on the original book by David McKee © 1999, David McKee (1999, Scholastic Ltd). **The Penguin Group (UK)** for an extract and illustration from *101 things to do with a baby* by Jan Ormerod © 1984, Jan Ormerod (1984, Viking). **The Penguin Group (UK)** for an extract from *Hue Boy* by Rita Phillips Mitchell © 1992, Rita Phillips Mitchell (1992, Gollancz). **Peters Fraser Dunlop Group on behalf of The Estate of Hilaire Belloc** for an extract from 'Matilda Who Told Lies, and Was Burned to Death' by Hilaire Belloc from *Cautionary Tales for Children* by Hilaire Belloc © 1907, Hilaire Belloc. **Joan Poulson** for 'School break' by Joan Poulson from *Another second poetry book* compiled by John Foster © 1988, Joan Poulson (1988, Oxford University Press). **The Random House Group** for an extract and illustration from *Old Bear* by Jane Hissey © 1986, Jane Hissey (1986, Hutchinson Children's Books). **The Random House Group** for an extract from *The Patchwork Quilt* by Valerie Flournoy © 1985, Valerie Flournoy (1985, The Bodley Head). **Transworld Publishers** for an extract and illustration from *The Teddy Robber* by Ian Beck. Text and illustration © 1989, Ian Beck (1989, Doubleday). **Walker Books Ltd** for an extract from *Owl Babies* by Martin Waddell © 1992, Martin Waddell (1992, Walker Books Ltd). **Walker Books Ltd** for an extract and illustration from *Willy the Wimp* by Anthony Browne © 1984, Anthony Browne (1984, Julia Macrae Books). **Walker Books Ltd** for an extract and illustration from *Once there were giants* by Martin Waddell. Text © 1989, Martin Waddell. Illustration © Penny Dale (1989, Walker Books Ltd). **Walker Books Ltd** for an extract and one illustration from *Little Beaver and The Echo* by Amy MacDonald and Sarah Fox-Davis. Text © 1990, Amy MacDonald. Illustration © 1990, Sarah Fox-Davis (1990, Walker Books Ltd). **Walker Books Ltd** for an extract from *Happy Birth Day!* by Robie H. Harris © 1996, Robie H. Harris (1996, Walker Books Ltd). **The Watts Publishing Group Ltd** for an extract and illustration from *The world is full of babies* by Mick Manning and Brita Granström. Text © 1996, Mick Manning. Illustrations © 1996 Brita Granstrom (1996, Franklin Watts). **The Watts Publishing Group Ltd** for pages 21 and 22 from *I can cook* by Judy Bastyra © 1996, Judy Bastyra (1996, Franklin Watts).

Every effort has been made to trace copyright holders and the publishers apologise for any omissions.

Introduction

The new National Curriculum (2000) included, for the first time, a specific personal, social and health education with citizenship curriculum (PSHE and citizenship). Though non-mandatory at Key Stages 1 and 2, it is an important component of the education children receive in primary school, one for which OFSTED will be looking for evidence. This importance is reflected in its parallel presence in the Foundation Stage Guidelines as a major area of development.

The delivery of PSHE and citizenship in primary schools has always occurred to some extent, whether planned or unplanned. It is delivered through the taught curriculum and as an implicit part of the pastoral support and disciplinary systems in place in school. Many of the specific objectives in the PSHE and citizenship curriculum will be able to be matched to aspects of current medium- and short-term plans, especially in the Literacy Hour, RE, science, the humanities, and the creative and practical subjects, such as PE, music and art.

The demands of the new PSHE and citizenship syllabus

The PSHE and citizenship curriculum objectives for Key Stages 1 and 2, as set out in the curriculum guidelines, cover four main sections or themes:

◆ developing confidence and responsibility and making the most of abilities
◆ preparing to play an active role as citizens
◆ developing a healthy, safer lifestyle
◆ developing good relationships and respecting differences between people.

In addition, section 5, Breadth of opportunities, gives specific examples of the ways the objectives can be met.

The first section includes work on feelings, communication and upon building self-esteem, a prerequisite of effective learning. The second section contains a mixture of objectives centering upon the need for rules, the identification of right and wrong and the need to contribute to the school, the family and the local community. It covers responsibilities to others, including pets and emergent environmental issues. The third section is linked strongly with the science curriculum in that it focuses largely on the body. It requires children to make healthier lifestyle choices, to keep safe and to understand the needs of the young and old. It also encourages children to seek out appropriate adult help when in difficulties. The fourth section focuses upon equal opportunities issues and on understanding the impact of personal actions, words and behaviour upon others. It requires the skills to listen to others and to be able to work and play with others cooperatively. It introduces the problem of bullying and identifies the difference between bullying and teasing.

Teaching PSHE and citizenship through texts

The National Literacy Strategy is a particularly valuable means by which PSHE and citizenship can be cultivated. The use of texts, particularly those that stimulate the imagination and allow rehearsal of situations in the children's minds, enables the development of specific concepts and skills. Discussion of motives and character, of prediction and the consequences of plot development, and the building up of an *emotional* vocabulary all help children to recognise feelings and dangers, say what they need clearly, be able to listen and begin to compromise. The National Literacy Strategy also encourages children to have the confidence to speak out, to enter into collective activities and to organise and manage their own learning. It is only a short step from the current work being undertaken in the Literacy Hour, promoting high literacy standards, to using that work explicitly to develop children as individuals and members of society. It can be fun and creative too!

Achieving the PSHE and citizenship syllabus objectives through this book

This book aims to provide practical support for the class teacher by providing a bank of texts and related activities that can be incorporated into the Literacy Hour, and other cross-curricular work, to deliver the PSHE and citizenship objectives. Although the material is organised into thematic chapters, the holistic nature of PSHE and citizenship means that these divisions can be treated as guidelines only. Certain texts will have activities that address several themes. This flexibility in use will increase the book's value as a tool for your teaching.

Easy access is provided to explicit PSHE and citizenship objectives and activities to directly meet them. The chapters are organised around key PSHE themes: Ourselves, Families, Friendship, Respecting differences, Keeping safe, Keeping healthy and Citizenship. Each chapter contains a series of texts of differing genres, followed by ideas for discussing the text. These include reference to literacy points as well as syllabus objectives within a focused textual framework. Identification of key vocabulary for each text is given, as well as ideas for displaying work undertaken by the children during the activities, or other display ideas to reinforce the text's main concepts. This is followed by a series of suggested PSHE and citizenship activities. Further literacy ideas conclude the examination of each text, to support independent activities and guide writing tasks. The appropriate PSHE and citizenship objectives met through the work are given each time. These objectives can be achieved through both completion of the activities themselves and as a product of the process of organised sharing, cooperation and discussion necessary for the achievement of the activities.

The stress on the development of generic skills and attitudes within the syllabus means that virtually all the texts address automatically the following common objectives:
- ◆ To share opinions on things that matter and be able to explain points of view (1b).
- ◆ To recognise, name and deal with feelings in a positive way (1c).
- ◆ To take part in discussions with one other person and the whole class (2a).
- ◆ To listen to other people, and play and work cooperatively (4b).

These four are to be taken as common to all tasks in addition to those objectives named under each text and are therefore not specified each time.

The following grid, on pages 7–8, summarises the themes, objectives and genre of each text for ease and speed of use. The activities are appropriate for both year groups, though inevitably you will need to adapt the ideas to suit the particular abilities and stages of development of the children in your classes.

PSHE and citizenship work offers the chance to recapture some of those enjoyable, interesting and creative dimensions in the children's work. Enjoy it.

EXTRACT	GENRE	PSHE & CITIZENSHIP LEARNING OBJECTIVES	LITERACY LEARNING OBJECTIVES	PAGE
Goldilocks and the three bears	Traditional story	1a, 2b, 2c, 2d, 2f, 4a, 5a, 5g	◆ To re-enact a story in role-play. ◆ To write simple newspaper reports	77
Louis Braille	Information text	2e, 3d, 4c, 5e	◆ To write a poem in response to a text. ◆ To write information texts.	80
The tenth good thing about Barney	Narrative fiction	1d, 3d, 4d, 5a, 5b	◆ To investigate different ways of presenting information about characters.	83
Amazing Grace	Narrative fiction from a range of cultures	1a, 2f, 4a, 4c, 5b	◆ To write simple evaluations of books read and discussed giving reasons. ◆ To plan and write a structured story.	86

Keeping safe

EXTRACT	GENRE	PSHE & CITIZENSHIP LEARNING OBJECTIVES	LITERACY LEARNING OBJECTIVES	PAGE
Matilda Who Told Such Dreadful Lies…	Rhyming poem with a moral tale by a significant author	1a, 2c, 2d, 3g, 4a, 5h	◆ To write a simple set of instructions. ◆ To use simple poetry structures to write a humorous poem. ◆ To look at different spellings of words with ow sounds.	90
Safety signs	Labels and signs with captions	2e, 2h, 3a, 3f, 3g, 4a, 4d, 5h	◆ To make a class poster about safety. ◆ To investigate antonyms.	93
Humpty Dumpty	Nursery rhyme	2c, 3a, 3g, 4d, 5a, 5d	◆ To rewrite a story from another point of view. ◆ To write a poem with an alternate line rhyming scheme.	96
Keeping safe in the home	Explanation text	1a, 2c, 3a, 3f, 3g, 5a, 5c, 5h	◆ To identify the key features of an explanatory text. ◆ To investigate the vowel phoneme oi.	99
Owl Babies	Picture book narrative fiction	2f, 3g, 4d	◆ To write a set of rules. ◆ To use a variety of sources to gather information and write a non-fiction text.	102

Keeping healthy

EXTRACT	GENRE	PSHE & CITIZENSHIP LEARNING OBJECTIVES	LITERACY LEARNING OBJECTIVES	PAGE
Willy the Wimp	Narrative fiction by a well-known author	1e, 2b, 3a, 3d, 3e, 5b, 5d	◆ To use word endings -ed(past tense) and -ing (present tense).	106
You are what you eat!	Explanation text	1a, 1d, 1e, 2b, 2c, 2e, 3a, 5d, 5g	◆ To design a leaflet about healthy eating. ◆ To investigate simple differences between Standard English and dialect. ◆ To look at nouns and adjectives linked to food.	109
Pasta house	Instructional text	1a, 1b, 1e, 2b, 2c, 2d, 3b, 5a, 5h	◆ To investigate the imperative tense used in recipes. ◆ To investigate the i before e except after c rule.	112
Hair	Humorous poetry	1a, 2b, 2c, 3a	◆ To make a collection of words with the rime air in them. ◆ To write their own poems using the poem's structure (rhyming couplets).	116
Getting ready for bed	Non-fiction procedural text	1a, 2c, 2e, 3a, 3b, 3e	◆ To write a simple account. ◆ To use diagrams and labels to write instructions. ◆ To use word endings -ed(past tense) and -ing (present tense).	119

Citizenship

EXTRACT	GENRE	PSHE & CITIZENSHIP LEARNING OBJECTIVES	LITERACY LEARNING OBJECTIVES	PAGE
The Three Pigs	Re-telling of a familiar story	1a, 1d, 2b, 2c, 2g, 3g, 4a, 5c, 5g, 5h	◆ To make a collection of verbs to describe talking and to learn to use some of these in their own writing.	123
The Three Little Wolves and the Big Bad Pig	Reworking of a familiar tale	1a, 1d, 2c, 4a, 4e	◆ To write their own ending for a familiar story. ◆ To identify and discuss characterisation.	126
The Teddy Robber	Fantasy with a familiar setting	1a, 2c, 2d, 2h, 4a, 5a, 5d, 5f, 5g, 5h	◆ To write invitations. ◆ To plan menus.	129
Citizen rap	Modern rhyming poem/song	1a, 1e, 2b, 2c, 2d, 2e, 2g, 2h, 4a, 5b, 5g	◆ To write a rap-style poem. ◆ To look at words with the rime ap in them.	132
Mine!	Fiction with a familiar setting	1a, 1d, 2c, 2d, 2e, 4a, 4d	◆ To represent outlines of story plot using a storyboard. ◆ To investigate the use of an exclamation marks.	135
I want a pet!	Play	1a, 1e, 2c, 2e, 4a, 5a	◆ To become aware of character and dialogue by reading aloud plays. ◆ To write simple riddles.	138
Infant School Disaster	Humorous poem	1a, 2c, 2d, 4a	◆ To investigate the digraph sh. ◆ To write an additional verse to the poem in the author's style.	142

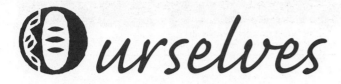 # Ourselves

Young children are often egocentric and very interested and concerned about themselves, their feelings, their relationships and growing up. They are fascinated about how they have changed from being a baby and what will happen as they get older. This chapter will help children focus on themselves and their personal development from birth to present day. It will encourage children to look at their relationships with others and to reflect upon their early experiences and how they have grown and changed.

Within PSHE and citizenship at Key Stage 1 children begin to look at sex education. This needs to be dealt with sensitively and cautiously. Some of the texts in this section will raise questions for children about where babies come from. Remember that children only need a simple answer to begin with that gives limited information. Children will ask the next question when they are ready for more information. For example, when asked *Where does a baby come from?* you could explain that the baby grows inside the mummy in *a warm safe place*. Some children might then ask how the baby gets out – a standard response then would be *through a special opening*. This level of explanation will be sufficient for most Key Stage 1 children and any further questions could be handled individually, or children's parents alerted to inquisitiveness. Consideration also needs to be given to the school's policy on sex education. Each individual school will have an agreed policy written by staff and governors about what, how and when sex education should be taught. At Key Stage 1 this is the beginning of a spiral curriculum which will develop over the next few years and how you deal with issues should be in accordance with this long-term plan.

The texts in this chapter also look at children's relationships with their friends and families, and encourage them to reflect on these from their own point of view.

Genre
procedural
text

101 Things to do with a Baby

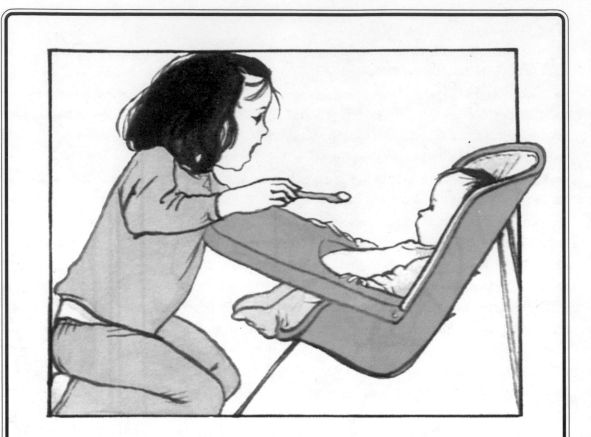

1. say good morning
2. play with baby before breakfast
3. put him in his special chair
4. give him cereal
5. and let him share your egg
6. better clean him up
7. let's do the washing
8. put it in the machine
9. add the soap powder
10. watch it whizz around

by Jan Ormerod

101 *Things to do with a Baby*

Display pictures and photographs of babies. Ask the children to bring in photographs of themselves as babies or of baby siblings.

PSHE and citizenship learning objectives

◆ To think about ourselves, learn from experiences and recognise what we are good at (1d).

◆ To realise that people and other living things have needs and that there are responsibilities to meet them (2e).

◆ To understand about belonging to various groups and communities, such as family (2f).

◆ To recognise the need to maintain personal hygiene (3b).

◆ To understand the process of growing from young to old and how people's needs change (3d).

◆ To understand that all household products can be harmful if not used properly (3f).

◆ To understand rules for, and ways of, keeping safe (3g).

◆ To feel positive about ourselves (5b).

Vocabulary

Baby, looking after, clean, dirty, young.

Discussing the text

◆ Read the text with the children and ask what they notice about the way the text is organised. Have they seen this organisation before? Where? (The instructions for a board game, instructions around the school, perhaps in the cookery or art area, in a recipe.) Discuss with them why the text is written like this.

◆ Ask the children what time of day they think it is in the text. What clues are there to tell them this? (Get them to focus on what is happening in the house.)

◆ Who do the children think the main characters in the story are? Ask them who is being looked after and why.

PSHE and citizenship activities

◆ Discuss with the children how the baby is being looked after in the text. Make a list on a flip chart of the children's suggestions of the ways the baby needs to be cared for and discuss why. Augment this list with the children's own ideas and experiences of how they know babies need caring for. The children can make their own 'How to look after a baby' poster using the ideas collected.

◆ Return to points seven to ten in the text. Can the children tell you what is happening here? Discuss with them who has a washing machine or who visits the laundrette. What does the washing machine do? Do they know how people cleaned clothes before there were washing machines? Discuss how nice it is to have clean clothes to keep us warm.

◆ Discuss with the children other ways in which they look after themselves and babies, for example washing and bathing, brushing their teeth and hair. Divide the children into groups and get each group to write instructions for an everyday activity linked to looking after themselves. Make a display of these.

◆ With the class make a list of the things they do every morning when they get up. Point out that most people do the same sorts of things but in different orders and assure the children that individual differences are fine. Get each individual to make a timeline for a morning's activities, from waking to arriving at school.

◆ Ask children to bring in photos of themselves as babies. They can use these to make individual books about how they have grown and changed. Ask what they do for themselves now that they couldn't when they were babies. (Dress themselves, feed themselves, walk and talk.) Get the children to draw the activities they can do now and label them, and make a display of these.

◆ Make a class book about looking after babies by getting different groups to prepare a page about a specific way to help babies. Have a collection of non-fiction books that the children can look at to help them do this.

◆ Make a baby-clinic role-play area and display the children's books and posters there. Provide a variety of activities and equipment that would be used to look after babies, such as nappies, a baby bath, bottles and so on.

Further literacy ideas

◆ Focus on the organisation of this text and other procedural texts. Identify with the children how a procedural text needs to be organised and how it is written (for example, *put him…, give her…, add the…*).

◆ Collect a series of instructions from children's games, TV manuals, and so on. Show these to the class and on a flip chart make a list together of the types of words and phrases found in them. Display the instructions in the writing area.

◆ If your school has a washing machine, show groups of children how to use it and then ask them to write a set of instructions about how to do this using some of the words already collected. These could be displayed next to the washing machine.

◆ Ask the children to write a set of instructions outlining how to use or do something in either the classroom, at home or in school (for example, how to use the tape recorder to listen to a story, how to keep the cloakroom tidy, how to wash their hands for lunch).

◆ Using a photo of themselves as a baby get the children to make a table of the similarities and differences between themselves now and how they were then.

The world is full of babies!

Genre
non-fiction
report

All over the earth, babies are sleeping. You slept cosy in a cot with blankets and gentle music.

If you were a bat baby you'd sleep upside down, hanging on with tiny fingernails in a draughty old roof space…

If you were a sea bird chick you'd sleep through a storm perched on a cliff high above the sea…

If you were a whale baby you'd float alongside mum with all the sea for a bed and whale song for a lullaby…

by Mick Manning and Brita Granström

The world is full of babies!

Display pictures or books showing the homes of different animals and birds with their young in them.

PSHE and citizenship learning objectives

◆ To recognise likes and dislikes (1a).
◆ To recognise choices can be made (2c).
◆ To realise that people and other living things have needs and that there are responsibilities to meet them (2e).
◆ To understand about belonging to various groups and communities such as family (2f).
◆ To make simple choices that improve health and well-being (3a).
◆ To understand the process of growing from young to old and how needs change (3d).
◆ To recognise that family and friends should care for each other (4d).

Vocabulary

Sleep, safe, cosy, gentle, draughty, storm, perched, lullaby.

Discussing the text

◆ Read the first paragraph with the children and encourage them to talk about the information there and the pictures. Ask them which words in the text make the cot sound a nice safe place to be.
◆ Ask the children what they slept in when they were babies and where. There will be many variations. Assure them that all are equally good as long as the baby is safe. Discuss with the children what makes a baby safe when sleeping, for example no danger of them falling out, keeping them warm, making sure they won't get stuck in the covers. (You may need to be sensitive to any children who have experienced a cot death in the family. Assure them that this is not anyone's fault but that however safe we try to be with babies some are just not well enough to live, that this does occasionally happen and no one knows why.)
◆ Read the other paragraphs with the class, one by one, discussing the individual cases in terms of safety, warmth, and so on. Compare the differences between young in the wild and domestic pets. Try to get the children to think about how the mothers or fathers of the sea bird or whale may feel. (For example, how does the mother whale know her baby won't get swept away by the sea?)
◆ Ask the children if they know about any other creatures and how they care for their young. Have they seen any at a zoo? Have they any pets that have had babies? Have they had a bird's nest in the garden or seen frogspawn in a pond?

PSHE and citizenship activities

◆ As a class, write a questionnaire for the children to take home to find out: where they slept as a baby, who put them to bed, how old they were when they slept in their own room, where they slept during the day. Collect the questionnaires back (these can also be used for maths activities) and get the children to write their own account of where they slept as a baby, who put them to bed, and so on from the information gathered on the questionnaire.
◆ Discuss with the children where they sleep now. In pairs, get them to share descriptions of their bedrooms, why they like them, who they share them with and so on. Get them to individually draw pictures of their bedrooms, label these and write a small explanation about them.

◆ Show the children a collection of bedroom ideas from catalogues and magazines. After a discussion about what the different bedrooms are like, ask them to plan and design their ideal bedroom. What would they have in it? What colour would it be? They can draw or cut out pictures to do this. Display these with the drawings and descriptions of their real bedrooms. How different are they? Children could use their plans to make a 3-D model of their ideal bedroom for a doll or play people.

◆ Using non-fiction texts, the Internet and CD-ROMs, invite the children to find out how different animals and birds look after their young. Tell them they are going to use the information to make a class book about animals and how their babies are cared for. This could be done using a word-processing package and importing pictures from the Internet or a CD-ROM, or scanning in photos and pictures. (Be aware of any copyright issues here – check your school's position.)

◆ Children could paint or draw pictures of animals and birds and their young based on the information collected in the activity above. They could then use the information and pictures to make a display or plan a class assembly.

◆ Invite a local Health Visitor, parent and baby into the classroom to talk to the children about how babies need to be looked after.

◆ Ask the children to write a set of instructions for going to bed based on their personal experiences. Are there any differences between weekdays and weekends and holidays? Why do they think this is? This is an ideal opportunity to talk with the children about their fears about being in the dark at bedtime. This should be done in a caring, sensitive way. Many children may have night-lights or other things that make them feel safe. Read *The Owl Who Was Afraid of the Dark* by Jill Tomlinson to them. This will provide many opportunities for further discussion in this area.

◆ Discuss with the children why sleep is so important for our bodies and especially for growing children. Talk about how they feel when they are tired and when they are wide awake. Help the children to realise the importance of sleep for healthy bodies and minds.

Further literacy ideas

◆ After a visit from a local Health Visitor and a parent with a new baby, ask the children to write a letter of thanks to them. Use school letter-headed paper explaining why this is appropriate for a formal letter. Allow the children to decide whether it will be handwritten or word-processed. This could be done as individuals or in pairs.

◆ Ask the children to write a report about the visit by the Health Visitor and new parent. Show them other reports in the local paper to find out how they are written. Provide a worksheet which scaffolds the report for younger or less able children.

◆ Investigate words associated with feeling safe and cared for with the class. Start with those used in the text, such as *lullaby* and *gentle*, and then explore words the children associate with feeling safe and being cared for. Make a list on a flip chart to display. Some children could use a thesaurus to find additional words. Then, as a class, make a list of antonyms to display alongside the safe words.

◆ Ask the children to make a list of instructions for caring for a baby using information gathered from visitors and non-fiction texts.

◆ Make a class poster about how to keep a baby safe using information from other PSHE activities.

◆ Make a worksheet or game from the text that gives the children an animal or bird and a matching sentence describing how the young of that species are cared for. Tell the children they have to find the matching pairs, for example *baby bat/sleeps upside down in a draughty old roof space* or *whale baby/float alongside mum with all the sea for a bed*, and so on. Making the sentences on laminated card will enable them to be used many times or displayed as an activity.

Genre
*story with
rhyme and
repetition*

Once there were giants

When I went to school
I'd got bigger by then.
Mum had to leave at
a quarter to ten and
she didn't come back
for a long, long time.
I didn't shout and
I didn't scream.
She came for me at
a quarter to three.

The one on Mum's knee is me.

by Martin Waddell
illustrated by Penny Dale

Once there were giants

Make a collection of other texts that have passages describing children's first days at school. Display these for class use.

PSHE and citizenship learning objectives

◆ To recognise likes and dislikes, and what is fair and unfair (1a).

◆ To think about ourselves and learn from experiences (1d).

◆ To agree and follow rules for the group and classroom (2d).

◆ To understand about belonging to various groups and communities, such as school (2f).

◆ To recognise how behaviour affects other people (4a).

◆ To recognise that family and friends should care for each other (4d).

◆ To develop relationships through work and play (5f).

◆ To be able to ask for help (5h).

Vocabulary

Starting, feelings, anxious, worried, excited, lonely, lost, overwhelmed.

Discussing the text

◆ Read the text with the children all the way through, then on a second reading ask them to really think about what the text is describing. Discuss with the children what they think the poem is about. Go through each line and discuss what each part means.

◆ Having established that the text is about a child's first day at school, ask if any of them remember their first day at school. What memories do they have?

◆ Ask the children what routines they have when they are brought to school now. Together, consider what rules the class and school have. Focus, for example, on whether parents come into the classroom or children are left at the door, and so on. What do the children think about these rules? Would they prefer something different to happen? How do they think their mums and dads felt leaving them on their first day, and how do they think they feel when they bring them now? Discuss also what happens at hometime. Talk about the safety aspect of someone picking the children up from school. Ask them to think about what rules are in place to keep them safe at hometime.

◆ Discuss with the children what activities they remember doing from their first few days at school. Can they remember if they enjoyed starting school or not?

◆ Ask the children to think about how the child in the text feels. What lines suggest the child is not very happy? (*I didn't shout* and *I didn't scream*.) Look at these lines closely. Why do the children think the child is saying what they did not do, rather than what they did do? (The child is trying to be positive and brave about school. She feels like she should like it even though she didn't really.)

◆ Ask the children how they think the child feels in the last line of the text. (The child feels safe back on her mum's knee.) Ask them to suggest why they think this. Why is the text separated? Explain that this is a way of emphasising the line.

PSHE and citizenship activities

◆ Focus the children on the feelings of the child in the text at the beginning and end of their first day. Discuss times when the children have felt unhappy or worried but have not been able to talk about it.

Assure them that this happens to us all at times and is very brave, but there are times when we need to let people know we are worried so we can talk about it and feel better.

◆ Invite the teacher who taught the children in the Nursery or Reception class to come and share the children's memories of when they started school.

◆ Discuss the idea with the class that it is because the child in the text does not know what to expect that they feel anxious. Talk about experiences the children have had when they have been anxious about something, for example a visit or going to a new activity, and then thoroughly enjoyed it. Discuss with them times when you have felt like this so they know everyone has times like this and it is OK. Talk about strategies that could help the children cope positively with these situations, such as the activity will only last for one hour and then someone will be back for them, or they do not have to join in but can opt out if they don't like an activity.

◆ What do the children think their mums and dads do while they are at school? Some children may be anxious because they think their mothers, fathers or carers will be lonely. Get them to ask at home about a typical day for Mum, Dad or their carer when they are at school. Make lists of what the adults do when the children are at school on a flip chart.

◆ Investigate who brings each of the children to school and record the information on the flip chart. Stress to the class that it is often not Mum, as in the text, but that dads, grandparents, childminders, brothers, sisters, link-club workers, and so on can bring them. Make a class graph for each day of the week to show the information recorded. Some children will have routines of different people for different days of the week and individuals can make a timetable to show this. The same could be done with hometime arrangements.

◆ Look again at the last line of text with the children. How does sitting on Mum's knee make the child feel? Talk about special things the children like doing with their parents or carers (a story at bedtime, a cuddle, having their hair stroked, curling up in front of the TV). (Be aware that in extreme circumstances child abuse issues may arise here, talk to the designated person in school about this if you have any concerns.)

◆ As a class get the children to write a 'Welcome to our school' booklet to send out to children who will start school in September.

Further literacy ideas

◆ Give each child a long strip of paper. Ask them to draw a comic strip showing what they do from getting up to arriving at school. Tell them to put in speech bubbles to show what different people are saying. Use one of the children's examples to look at how the text in the speech bubbles is written.

Focus on the use of speech marks by rewriting the child's morning activities as a textual account. More able children can try this in pairs or individually using their own cartoon strips.

◆ With the class look at the rhymes in the text and point out that they are not at the end of the line as expected. In groups, get the children to highlight the rhyming words.

◆ As a shared writing activity write a class poem about the routines of the day. Try to get the children to write this with rhyming couplets or with alternate lines rhyming.

◆ In pairs, get the children to write acrostic poems about coming to school or hometime. Display these with the graphs from the activity showing who brings or collects the children from school.

◆ Ask the children to write about a significant adult in their life. Get them to describe the adult, what it is that makes them special and what they particularly like doing with them.

The Quarrel

Genre
poem with familiar setting

I quarrelled with my brother,

I don't know what about,

One thing led to another

And somehow we fell out.

The start of it was slight,

The end of it was strong,

He said he was right,

I knew he was wrong!

We hated one another.

The afternoon turned black.

Then suddenly my brother

Thumped me on the back,

And said, "Oh, *come* along!

We can't go on all night –

I was in the wrong."

So he was in the right.

by Eleanor Farjeon

The Quarrel

Display pictures of brothers and sisters, drawn by those children who have them, with descriptions. Those who don't have a sibling should draw a cousin or a best friend.

PSHE and citizenship learning objectives

◆ To recognise what is fair and unfair, and what is right and wrong (1a).

◆ To think about ourselves, learn from our experiences and recognise what we are good at (1d).

◆ To take part in simple debate about topical issues (2b).

◆ To recognise choices can be made (2c).

◆ To understand about belonging to various groups and communities, such as family and school (2f).

◆ To recognise how behaviour affects other people (4a).

◆ To recognise that family and friends should care for each other (4d).

◆ To learn to develop relationships through work and play (5f).

◆ To consider social and moral dilemmas in everyday life (5g).

Vocabulary

Quarrel, brother, sister, slight, strong, forgive, agree to disagree.

Discussing the text

◆ Read the poem with the children and discuss with them what they think it is about. Ask them who they think could be writing the poem and introduce the vocabulary *sister* and *brother*. Ask who has a brother or a sister, who has more than one, or none. Get individuals to share a little information about their siblings. Do they like having brothers and sisters? Do those that do not have one want one? Why or why not? Try to encourage a simple debate about the pros and cons of each situation.

◆ Look at the first verse with the children. Focus on the lines that end in *slight* and *strong*. Ask the children if they know what these words mean, and point out that *slight* is often used to describe people who are small and quite weak, where *strong* is equated with being powerful. Ask them to suggest why the argument in the poem is described as starting slight and becoming strong. Develop the idea of the argument starting over a small thing and building up until it was really bad. Have any of the children experienced falling out over something that started as a small disagreement and finished as a really big row? Perhaps you could relate a personal experience to them to illustrate this point. Why has the author used the words *slight* and *strong* in the text in this way? Introduce very simply the idea of using types of figurative language in poetry.

◆ Focusing on the second verse, talk about the metaphor of the afternoon turning black. Do the children think it really did? What is the writer trying to do by using that type of language? Explain that the afternoon was spoilt by the argument just like a sunny day is spoilt by dark rain clouds.

◆ Ask the children how the poem ended. What happened between the two children? Were they brothers, or a brother and sister? Can they find any clues in the text? Who do they think was the most sensible? Look at the spoken text of the brother, pointing out the speech marks. Try to get the children to understand the last two lines by discussing the different meanings of right and wrong in both verses. Discuss with them the concept of admitting they are wrong and how difficult this is.

Suggest that other people should respect this and forgive them.

◆ Look at the use of exclamation marks in the text. When are they used? Why are they used? (For example, *I knew he was wrong!* – the exclamation mark is used to show indignation.)

PSHE and citizenship activities

◆ Work with a group of children to develop a role-play of the first verse of the poem. Show this to the rest of the class and then divide the class into two groups, giving each group a particular character to 'stick up' for. Get each group to show their scenario to the other. Then, in pairs, ask the children to discuss why this particular character was in the right. (This will depend on what the children think the quarrel was about and the ideas they come up with.) Get the pairs within the group to feed back their ideas and make a list for each group. Present the findings of each group to the whole class. Discuss again the rights and wrongs of the situation and how we are all entitled to points of view. Introduce the concept of accepting that not everyone will always see things as they do and at times they have to learn to agree to disagree.

◆ Ask the children to write about their brothers and sisters – who they are, what they look like and what they like and dislike doing with them. For those who do not have siblings ask them to write about why they would or would not want one: What do they think they would do with a sibling? (For example, play, eat tea together, have someone to talk to.) What would be the advantages and disadvantages of having one?

◆ Discuss with the children how we can love people but may not get on with them really well all the time – there may be things that people say or do that we do not like. Explain that we all get jealous at times and lose our tempers, but it does not stop others caring for us and loving us. Encourage them to share any experiences they may have had like this with family or friends so they realise it is normal to fall out, emphasise that it is how we deal with it afterwards that matters.

◆ In pairs, ask the children to make a poster suggesting ways of making up after an argument. Ask them to include ideas of things to do and things to say. Discuss how difficult it is to forgive.

◆ Get the children to write a card or letter to someone that they have quarrelled with recently explaining why they were naughty or got cross, how they felt afterwards and explaining what they want to happen now.

◆ In groups, ask the children to develop a role-play that shows both conflict and resolution. More able children could show two versions of this – a resolved and an unresolved ending.

Further literacy ideas

◆ Get the children to look at antonyms that they can find for words within the text, for example *brother/sister, back/front, right/wrong, slight/strong, out/in*.

◆ Ask the children to write pairs of sentences using antonyms for sentences in the poem, for example *he thumped me on the back/I poked him on his front*. Use the individual pairs of sentences to make a matching reading game (matching opposite sentences), or turn them into a class poem and display.

◆ Look at the root and suffix in *quarrel* and *quarrelled* with the children. Make a collection of other words that double the final consonant when adding *-ed* and ones that don't (for example, *grab/grabbed, talk/talked*) and investigate why. Explain to the children that the final consonant is doubled when the root of the word ends in vowel–consonant–vowel.

◆ The children can practise writing exclamation marks and using them correctly within sentences. These could be linked to what we might say when describing an argument, for example *'I hate you!' Mark shouted.* Some children could also use this activity to put in speech marks.

Family tree

Rebecca Jones
(Great-granny)

David Smith
(Great-grandad)

Anne Smith
(Granny)

John Field
(Grandad)

Robert Bank
(Dad)

Susan Field
(Mum)

Amy Bank
(Daughter)

Richard Bank
(Son)

Family tree

Display a collection of old things that may belong to a granny or great-granny (such as glasses, a walking stick, an old book, an old teddy, a hat, old-fashioned shoes and a handbag).

PSHE and citizenship learning objectives

◆ To think about ourselves, learn from our experiences and recognise what we are good at (1d).

◆ To take part in a simple debate about topical issues (2b).

◆ To agree and follow rules for the group and classroom, and understand how rules help them (2d).

◆ To understand about belonging to various groups and communities, such as family and school (2f).

◆ To understand what improves and harms their local, natural and built environments and about some of the ways people look after them (2g).

◆ To realise that money comes form different sources and can be used for different purposes (2i).

◆ To understand the process of growing from young to old and how people's needs change (3d).

Background notes

A family tree shows the history of the parents, grandparents and relations of people within the family. It is organised in a special way showing who married who and children they had. In this family tree we are focusing on grandparents and great-grandparents.

Vocabulary

Great-granny, great-grandad, grandparents, family tree, generation, mother, father, child.

Discussing the text

◆ Explain what a family tree is (a picture showing the relationship between a family that is called a tree because of all the different branches).

◆ Look at the family tree and picture with the children and ask questions about them such as *Who is this? Who is ......'s grandparents?* Explain to the class how a family tree is read. Can they match each person on the tree to a person in the picture? What evidence do they need to look for in order to do this? (It is linked to age, dress, size, and so on.) Focus on the family tree and on Granny. Ask the children how we know which is Granny. (Discuss what a granny is.) Which do they think is granny in the other picture? What about great-granny? Introduce the term *generation* to the children. Ask who has two or three generations in their families. Children will need help deciding this and may need to ask at home.

◆ Ask the children to think about their granny or older person in their family. Do they look like the granny in this picture? What do their grannies look like? Focus on their hair, skin, clothes and shoes.

◆ Discuss with the children the sorts of things they like doing with their grannies or older relative. What do they think makes grannies special? (For example, treats, staying over, babysitting, baking cakes.)

PSHE and citizenship activities

◆ Investigate other simple family trees with the children. Start by sharing one of your own, going back to your grandparents or great-grandparents. Focus this very much on your relationship to everyone else and keep it simple. Choose one child to draw a family tree on a flip chart as a whole-class activity to demonstrate how to do it. Individual children can then draw their own family trees for their immediate family, including pictures and names. Younger children will need a framework to help them to do this. The finished family trees can then be displayed.

◆ Ask the children to write about a grandparent or an older family relative. Tell them they should include in this a description of what their chosen person looks like, what activities they do together and why they are a special member of the family. Are there any routines that happen when the children visit this person or visa versa? Share with them your experiences about a grandparent.

◆ Ask the children to think about what they did with their grandparents or elderly relatives when they were younger. What memories do they have of being young? The children can write about these and illustrate the sentences. These can be made into a class book called *When we were young*.

◆ Ask the children to bring two photographs of themselves into school – one when they were younger and one of them more recently. Make these into a *Guess who we are!* display.

◆ Use recent photographs of the children to make individual passports. Include personal details inside this document about their date of birth, height, weight, colour of their hair, colour of their eyes, names of their parents, and so on.

Further literacy ideas

◆ Look at other texts with the children that describe people talking about when they were younger, for example *When We Were Young* by AA Milne.

◆ Discuss with the children the sorts of things they like to do when they are not at school. Individuals could write descriptions of how they like to spend their time. Make this into a class book.

◆ Make a collection of words to describe being young, for example *little*, *youngest*, *small*, *tiny*.

◆ Look with the children at similar words for granny and granddad, for example *nana*, *grumpy*, *gramps*, *nanny*.

Happy Birth Day!

Genre
narrative
non-fiction

I'll never ever forget the moment you were born. Out pushed your head covered with wet and shiny hair. Then the rest of your wet and slippery body slid out and the midwife caught you with both hands.

Suddenly there you were – a whole new person, our baby! We saw all of you from head to toe and we loved you the moment we saw you.

You let out a loud cry – about as loud as a puppy dog howling at the moon. It was hard to believe that someone so tiny and new in the world could cry so loudly. But you did.

Your cry filled your lungs with air and you took your very first breath. Even though you were only a few seconds old, you were breathing on your own.

by Robie H Harris

■ SCHOLASTIC

Happy Birth Day!

Make a collection of pictures and information books that show young babies and explain simply about babies (check the contents of any books used first in case there is any explicit information you may not want the children to have at this stage).

PSHE and citizenship learning objectives

◆ To think about ourselves (1d).
◆ To realise that people and other living things have needs (2e).
◆ To understand the process of growing from young to old and how people's needs change (3d).
◆ To know the names of the main parts of the body (3e).

Background notes

The first paragraph of this extract raises the issue of where babies come from and how they are born. All children should be aware that the baby grows in the mummy's tummy and is then born. You do not need to go into any more detail with Key Stage 1 children unless your school policy on sex education has made specific plans to do so. If you do not feel confident discussing the first paragraph with the children omit it and read from paragraph two.

Vocabulary

Born, mummy, baby, breathing, lungs.

Discussing the text

◆ Read the text with the children and ask them what they think it is about. Consider with them, in a very simple way, where the baby has come from. If discussing the first paragraph, tell the children about how the mummy's tummy protects and looks after the unborn baby until it is big enough to be born.

◆ Ask the children to think about what a baby looks like when it is newly born. Collect some pictures and some newborn baby clothes to show how small a baby is. Discuss with the children how a baby needs a lot of caring for. Make a list on a flip chart of all the things a newborn baby needs doing for it and those things it can do on its own.

◆ Why do the children think the baby let out a loud cry when it was born? (Most will think it is unhappy, but in fact it is to get air into the lungs and help it start to breathe.) Explain that it has come from a warm safe place into what must seem a cold place. Also discuss the fact that this will help the baby to begin to breathe and that babies have to cry to let us know they need something as they can't talk.

PSHE and citizenship activities

◆ Focus the class on the baby taking its first breath. Discuss with the children what we do when we breathe. Ask: *What do our lungs do? Where are they?* Show the children a diagram to demonstrate how the lungs work or a model of the body. Get them to breathe deeply in and out and feel their rib cage. What do they notice? What is happening? (As we breathe in, the lungs fill with air and we can feel our ribs moving.) Talk to the children about what the ribs are and their function (protecting the lungs which are more delicate). Use a balloon to illustrate how the air fills up our lungs as we breathe in and how they shrink again when we breathe out. Why do the children think we breathe? Discuss with them how our bodies need oxygen and this is what we are breathing in. Simply explain that the oxygen passes into our bodies so we can live and be healthy. Set up activities to enable children to investigate what happens when we run, skip, and so on. Talk about what is happening when we get out of breath.

◆ Discuss with the class how important breathing is and how we can only breathe air. Explain that if water or other things stop the air getting into our lungs we could become very ill or die. Make links here with safety and being careful near water, such as swimming pools (because it can be dangerous to breathe in a lot of water). Also remind children of the dangers of playing with balloons and plastic bags (they can stop air from getting into our mouths and noses and into our lungs). The children could design posters about these safety issues.

◆ Discuss with the children what other things the baby needs to be able to do or have done for it to stay healthy, for example personal hygiene, nutrition and mental stimulation. Then ask the children to write about how to care for a newborn baby.

◆ Bring into the classroom a baby doll and things to look after it, for example a bath, bottle, nappy, and so on. Let the children practise caring for the baby using these in role-play situations.

◆ Ask a parent to bring in a baby to show the children what the baby can and cannot do, and how it needs to be cared for. This links with the work from the extract '101 Things to do with a Baby' on page 10.

◆ Look at a model of a baby and get the children to name the main parts of the body. Use the words to make a wordbank and individual children can then use this to draw and label their own picture of a baby.

◆ Ask the children to think and write about themselves when they were born. Who looked after them? What was done for them? Discuss with the children how much they have changed and all the things they have learned to do.

Further literacy ideas

◆ Ask the children to investigate and make a collection of synonyms to describe crying, such as *hollering, bawling,* and so on. Use these to display on a poster.

◆ Look at names of parts of the body with the children. Ask them to find other words that have the same pattern or rime, for example *hand/band* and *stand, foot/root* and *boot.* Investigate the sounds of the rime and sort the phonemes that make the rime. Investigate other endings that sound the same but are spelled differently, for example *foot* and *shut* (depending on accent!).

◆ Teach the children to spell some of the parts of the body.

◆ Comparing a baby with the children, look at words that describe size, weight and physical ability. Draw a picture of a baby and an average child of the children's age on the flip chart, and make a list of words under each to show the differences, for example *strong/weak, walk/crawl, tall/small.* This should help the children appreciate how much they have changed and developed as they've grown.

◆ Investigate superlatives with the children, such as *loudest* and *smallest.*

Families

Most children by the time they reach primary school have some notion of what 'family' means. However, awareness of the dynamics of family relationships, and the corresponding responsibilities and frustrations will not have been explored explicitly, though they will surely have been felt.

The concept of 'family' is so close to children that it is at once immediately familiar and also very sensitive. It makes it an ideal subject for younger children who need to operate directly from and within their experience, but has sufficient depth to enable successful work to be undertaken by older children.

Care and sensitivity are needed with those children with fractured family backgrounds, those in care or not living with their parents. It doesn't mean, however, that the concept cannot be addressed. The notion of family can include carers, siblings and the family of the school, the class and the group. Emphasising the positive and widest view of family can help children to feel accepted and supported.

The texts in this chapter address themes such as the nature, breadth and variations of the constituents of families. The elderly are included as a component of the family. This may be strange to children who live with daily contact with their parents and brothers and sisters only, but awareness of the extended family and of Gran and Grandad's valuable contribution to the group is important to cultivate. It is hoped that respect for the older members of society will be encouraged to counteract the imbalance towards the young felt amongst much of society today. The family too is seen as possessing a history that can be accessed and passed on.

The texts develop ideas associated with the tensions that can result within the family, especially with duties or responsibilities to help one another within the house. The desire to do what we want and not what someone else in the family wants is always present. Thus the concepts of mutual help, the family as a common enterprise and the need for practical caring of one another demand some reinforcement and explanation.

The texts also look at parental separation from the child, examined in relation to one parent having to work away from home. Strategies are given to help maintain contact with absent parents, and to both express and cope with the feeling of loss that can result from separation. Obviously these skills can be transferred to, and used by, the child experiencing parental separation through marital breakdown.

Finally, the family is looked at from the view of the child holidaying away from them, in this case on a short residential holiday organised by the school. It is increasingly the practice of schools to build in residential field trips for Year 2 children to give them the chance to develop independence away from the family. The piece enables children to be prepared for the fears and homesickness that they might experience and to learn about perseverance. Even if the Year 2 children are not going to go away with the school the piece can still be of relevance, as they may 'sleep over' with a friend.

Exploring situations and feelings through stories can genuinely prepare children for their own life experiences. Bringing feelings and fears about family out into the open makes them manageable, even if you are only five years old.

Family photographs

This is my family: Mum, me, Carl, Granny, Granddad and Auntie Margaret.

This is my family: Mum, Dad, me, Asha, Bharti, Uncle Naresh, Auntie Leela, Uncle Rajesh and Auntie Sumitra.

This is my family: Mum, Dad, Rosa, Carmel, 'Rob Roy' the dog and me.

This is my family: Mum, Dad, me, Grandpa, Grandma, Great-grandpa, Great-grandma and my cousin Chi Han.

This is my family: my foster mum, my foster dad, my brother Eddie, my sister Carly, me, my foster sister Lisa, my foster brother Paul.

This is my family: Nanny, Grandda, Matt and me.

Family photographs

Display photographs from the children of their own families, surrounded by the different names they use for the same member of a family, for example *granny, grandma*.

PSHE and citizenship learning objectives

◆ To take part in a simple debate about topical issues (2b).
◆ To understand about belonging to various groups and communities, such as family and school (2f).
◆ To identify and respect the differences and similarities between people (4c).
◆ To recognise that family and friends should care for each other (4d).
◆ To feel positive about ourselves (5b).

Background notes

Families can take many forms from the immediate to the extended. These photos are intended to allow you to explore with the children the idea of what is meant by family.

Vocabulary

Family, grandmother, granddad, auntie, uncle, brother, sister, foster, great-grandmother, photograph, family album.

Discussing the text

◆ Work through the first four families, asking children to read the captions with you.
◆ Ask the children what these photos have in common. (They are all pictures of families.) Where do they think they would see a photo like this at home? (In a family photograph album.) Show an example of a family album to the children.
◆ Discuss with the children what differences there are between the families. Ask them to comment on which generations are represented, the different sizes of the families, the names given by the child to their family members. Issues of race may come up. As long as these are suggested without racist overtones then accept that the families come from different cultures. If racist terms are used, stress that we don't use words like that and explain why we must treat everyone with respect. Being different is good.

◆ Look at the last two captions. Ask the children for suggestions about why there are no parents in either. If extreme reasons are given, offer more plausible and positive suggestions, for example Mum and Dad are working abroad or somewhere else in the country.
◆ Ask the children if they know what *foster* means. Write the word on a flip chart and then explain, referring to the children's examples. Explain the sorts of reasons why a child might be fostered, for example children whose parents are sick and cannot look after them for a little while, children whose parents are not around for some reason. Explain too that fostering means that children can live with a nice family who treat them as if they belong to them. (If you have a child

or children currently in care this might need great sensitivity or omission.)

◆ List the different names given for grandmother in the captions and record these on a flip chart. Ask children to tell you, one at a time, the name by which they call their gran. Tick the names if they are the same or add additional examples. Tally up the most popular.

◆ Discuss what is meant by *great-grandmother*. Use children to demonstrate four generations, using a shawl for Great-gran to wear, a hat for Gran, a baby doll wrapped for Mum to hold and a toy for the child to have. This can be done with male-linked objects too.

PSHE and citizenship activities

◆ Get each child to draw or paint a picture of their family, writing a caption as the text did.

◆ Ask the children to write a poem with a verse describing what they like about each of the members of their family. They should include a final verse about themselves, describing what they like about themselves.

◆ Divide the class into small groups and ask them to role-play a tableau for a formal family photo. The child can introduce his or her family to the class. Each character can tell the class what he or she does as part of that family, for example *I'm Holly's dad, I earn money to look after the family* or *I'm Holly's grandma, I look after the children when Mum and Dad want to go out for the night.*

◆ Get the children to draw a family tree with small pictures of heads for each member going back three or four generations. If children are struggling then they can draw just two generations, themselves and their parents.

◆ In groups of four get the children to play the *Happy Families* card game. Ensure rule abiding and organisation occurs.

Further literacy ideas

◆ In small groups, ask the children to list different names for grandfather, using the text and examples from their own group.

◆ Look at other examples of families with the class, for example families of animals, or families from soap operas or children's programmes.

◆ Ask the children to write a story about a special event in their family, for example Christmas or other religious festivals, birthdays, a christening.

◆ Make namecards using a word processor with each name of the children's family members on them. Members should be sorted in order of generation and stuck onto a piece of paper and connected to each other with lines.

◆ Find other books about families from the class library. Ask the children to choose a favourite for you to read to the class at story time.

◆ Find as many words as you can from the word *great-grandmother*, such as *rat*, *eat*, *ran* and *her*.

Family chores

PHOTOCOPIABLE

Genre
non-fiction list

Mum's chores

- cooking the meals
- cleaning the house
- shopping for food
- washing the clothes
- helping the children with their homework

Dad's chores

- emptying the rubbish bins
- hoovering
- filling the car with petrol
- cleaning the car
- ironing the clothes

Adam's chores

- cleaning his bedroom
- putting his clothes and shoes away in the cupboards
- picking up the towels in the bathroom
- sweeping the garden path
- feeding the rabbit every day

Sophie's chores

- tidying her bedroom
- bringing her dirty washing down
- putting her toys away in the box
- dusting the lounge
- cleaning out the rabbit once a week

Family chores

Display a list of classroom chores to be carried out by groups of children and illustrated by pictures of each group doing their jobs.

PSHE and citizenship learning objectives

◆ To recognise likes and dislikes, what is fair and unfair, and what is right and wrong (1a).

◆ To know how to set simple goals and reach them (1e).

◆ To recognise choices can be made (2c).

◆ To agree and follow rules for the group and classroom, and understand how rules help (2d).

◆ To realise that people and other living things have needs, and that there are responsibilities to meet them (2e).

◆ To understand about belonging to various groups and communities, such as family and school (2f).

◆ To contribute to the life of the class and the school (2h).

◆ To recognise how behaviour affects other people (4a).

◆ To acknowledge that family and friends should care for each other (4d).

◆ To consider moral and social dilemmas in everyday life, for example not being fair, not doing jobs but expecting others to do them (5g).

Vocabulary

List, chores, jobs, responsibility.

Discussing the text

◆ Begin by asking the children what the word *chore* means. If they find it easier to give examples rather than a definition, list these on a flip chart under the title *chore*.

◆ Discuss the negative connotation of the word *chore* – it is seen as hard and not enjoyable. Ask the children for a better name for these important tasks, for example *jobs*.

◆ Read the lists with the children or ask four children to represent the four characters and let them read out loud the chores.

◆ Ask the children why everyone in the house has these jobs to do. Why can't they all just do what they want and enjoy doing? Explain that each member of a family has a *responsibility* (put this word on the flip chart) to do their bit to make life easier for the family. If the jobs are shared then no one does too much and feels angry about this. Younger children might need to have this idea represented as *I do something to help you, you do something to help me*.

◆ Ask the children to give examples of chores they have to do in their house. Write a list on the flip chart of chores the children do collectively. Ask them which chores they least like and which they don't mind, then rank them in order from least to most minded. Ask them to explain why some tasks are better or worse than others, for example messy, hard or boring work.

PSHE and citizenship activities

◆ Ask the children to list the chores they do in their house and to illustrate with a picture of them doing their work.

◆ Discuss with the children what would happen if one of the members of the family in the text refused to do any of their jobs, for example failing to feed the rabbit. Ask groups to act out a scene

where this happens, each group taking a different list. Show how difficult it is when someone doesn't do as they should. Get each group to perform the scenes to the rest of the class.

◆ Ask groups of children to work on a second scene where the other three members of the family try to persuade the non-worker to do his or her jobs. Show the scenes to the class.

◆ Ask the children to write a story in which their brother or sister neglects their duties and asks them to do their chores for them for money. Will they do them or not? What do their parents say about that when they find out? What happens?

◆ Discuss with the children why it is important to do jobs even when we don't enjoy them. Explain that it is especially important if other people or animals are dependent on us doing our job.

◆ Talk with the class about the chores needed to be done in the classroom. List these on the flip chart. Ask groups of children to take responsibility for one or two of these for the term. Ask them to word-process their task (or tasks), and print out a copy for a display, whilst other members of the group can draw pictures of the group doing the tasks.

Further literacy ideas

◆ Collect words that describe the children's feelings around the word *chore*. Use these to write a poem called 'Chore'.

◆ Identify with the children the format for making a list, focusing on a sub-heading and short phrases one beneath the other.

◆ Compile other lists with the children, for example shopping lists, Christmas present lists, clothes lists for a holiday.

◆ Get each child to cut up the individual tasks on the lists of the text and rearrange them under Mum, Dad, Sophie and Adam. Each family member must have the same number of chores. The children can draw a picture with speech bubbles when one of the family gets their new list – what would they each say to their new list of chores?

◆ List on the flip chart words that rhyme with *chore*, for example *door, more, maw, jaw, poor, war, law, saw, sore*. Group the list into three different types of words: vowel–consonant–vowel words, such as *more* and *sore*; *aw* words, such as *law, saw, caw* and *raw*; and *or* words, such as *poor, door* and *or*.

The Patchwork Quilt

Genre
narrative
fiction

Grandma was sitting in her favourite spot – the big soft chair in front of the picture window. In her lap were scraps of material of all textures and colours. Tanya recognised some of them. The check was from Papa's old work shirt, and the red scraps were from the shirt Ted had worn that winter.

"What are you going to do with all that stuff?" Tanya asked.

"*Stuff?* These ain't stuff. These little pieces gonna make me a quilt, a patchwork quilt."

Tanya tilted her head. "I know what a quilt is, Grandma. There's one on your bed, but it's old and dirty and Mama can never get it clean."

Grandma sighed. "It ain't dirty, honey. It's worn, the way it's supposed to be."

Grandma flexed her fingers to keep them from stiffening. She sucked in some air and said, "My mother made me that quilt when I wasn't any older than you. But sometimes the old ways are forgotten."

Tanya leaned against the chair and rested her head on her grandmother's shoulder. Just then Mama walked in with two glasses of milk and some biscuits. She looked at the scraps of material that were scattered everywhere. "Grandma," she said, "I've just tidied this room, and now it's a mess."

"It's not a mess, Mama" Tanya said, through a mouthful of biscuit. "It's a quilt."

"A quilt! You don't need these scraps. I can get you a quilt," Mama said.

Grandma looked at her daughter and then turned to her grandchild. "Yes, your mama can get you a quilt from any department store. But it won't be like my patchwork quilt, and it won't last as long either."

Mama looked at Grandma, then picked up Tanya's empty glass and went to make lunch.

Grandma's eyes grew dark and distant. She turned away from Tanya and gazed out of the window, absentmindedly rubbing the pieces of material through her fingers.

"Grandma, I'll help you make your quilt," Tanya said.

"Thank you, honey."

"Let's start right now. We'll be finished in no time."

Grandma held Tanya close and patted her head. "It's gonna take quite a while to make this quilt, not a couple of days or a week – not even a month. A good quilt, a masterpiece…" Grandma's eyes shone at the thought. "Why, I need more material. More gold and blue, some red and green. And I'll need the time to do it right. It'll take me a year at least."

"A year!" shouted Tanya. "That's too long. I can't wait that long, Grandma."

Grandma laughed. "A year ain't that long, honey. Makin' this quilt gonna be a joy. Now run along and let Grandma rest." Grandma turned her head towards the sunlight and closed her eyes.

"I'm gonna make a masterpiece," she murmured, clutching a scrap of cloth in her hand just before she fell asleep.

by Valerie Flournoy

The Patchwork Quilt

Display quilt designs, a real quilt, books and photos of elderly people in family situations, story books about grandparents and families.

PSHE and citizenship learning objectives

◆ To understand belonging to various groups and communities, such as family and school (2f).

◆ To think about the ways people look after each other (2g).

◆ To know about the process of growing from young to old and how people's needs change (3d).

◆ To identify and respect the differences and similarities between people (4c).

◆ To know that family and friends should care for each another (4d).

Background notes

Valerie Flournoy's story *The Patchwork Quilt* is a rich story through which to explore the idea of memories and family history. It presents this Afro-Caribbean family in a contemporary European context and in its entirety touches on the place of grandparents within the family, their role as repositories of knowledge and memory, and the need for members of the family to support and help one another, specifically when Grandma becomes ill later in the story. This extract comes at the very beginning of the book and focuses on the pleasure that can be got from sharing a task.

Vocabulary

Grandma, granddad, quilt, special, memories, care, love, family.

Discussing the text

◆ Ask the children why they think Grandma was so fond of her old quilt. Was it because she had made it herself, or because the little bits of cloth reminded her of happy times in the past?

◆ Do the children have an old toy or piece of cloth, or item of clothing that is old, but they don't want to throw it away? Ask them why it is special to them.

◆ How do the children think that Tanya shows she loves and cares for her grandma? Ask them to find ways in the text. How do they show that they love their grannies and granddads, if they have them?

◆ Ask the children to say what they think Grandma and Tanya are going to do next.

◆ Discuss what Tanya does not like about the idea of making a quilt. What is Grandma's answer? Do the children think she is right – will Tanya enjoy working with her grandma for a whole year on a special quilt?

◆ Ask the children if they have worked with their grannies or granddads on any special project or job, such as working in the garden, or cooking or building something.

◆ Ask the children how old they think Grandma in the story is. How do they know?

PSHE and citizenship activities

◆ Hand out a worksheet that has on it a few joined pentangle shapes to look like a section of the quilt. In the centre pentangle ask the children to draw a picture of themselves, then around them in the connecting quilt sections to draw pictures of the people who love them and/or are special to them. (If there are children in local authority care in the class this must be considered.)

◆ Give out another blank worksheet to the children explaining that this time they should draw themselves in the centre and then put in each of the surrounding quilt sections items that are special to them, such as special toys, pictures or clothes. A few children can then be asked to explain to the class what objects they have chosen and why. A display can be made of these 'special quilts'.

◆ Make a class quilt. In groups of four (possibly friendship-based) get the children to make a quilt section using fabric of their choice (they could bring in a special piece of fabric from home that they wish to use for the quilt). Children should cut shapes using templates from scraps of fabric with an agreed colour base chosen by the group. This involves cooperative and collaborative work. Fabric sections could be sewn or, if preferred (for speed), stuck onto a stiff paper background. The group sections can then be displayed together as a big quilt on the display wall. Each group will tell the class why they chose the colours for their section.

◆ Ask an old person (for example, a grandparent, or even a great-grandparent) to come in and talk about special, old objects they have kept safe and what they mean to them. Encourage the children to listen and show respect for this visitor, and to write a letter of thanks afterwards.

◆ In a whole-class situation record on the flip chart the ways grandparents can help in a family. Children can role-play a family scene where a grandparent helps the family, for example babysitting, cooking a Sunday dinner, listening to the child read, looking after them after school. Encourage the children to act out their scenes to the class and receive applause. Point out the way that the grandparents helped to reaffirm the value and importance of these family members.

Further literacy ideas

◆ With the class, list gr words and qu words on a flip chart. Help the children put them into a wordbank.

◆ Ask the children to write about their special toy or item of clothing. Make these into a class book and display some examples.

◆ The children can write about a grandparent or a special person in their lives.

◆ Look at different words to describe colours, for example red can be *crimson*, *scarlet* or *cherry*. Create a class thesaurus with a colour chart.

◆ Record class suggestions for similes and metaphors linked to colour, for example *yellow is the sun in the sky*. These can be made into poems recorded on quilt segment shapes for display.

◆ Look at the way people use the past tense when recollecting memories and events from the past. Give the children some sentences using the present tense and ask them to change them into the past tense.

Hue Boy

Genre
narrative fiction depicting other cultures

Introduction to the text
This story is about a boy called Hue Boy who is the smallest child in his class and is desperate to grow taller. His mother seeks advice about how to make Hue Boy grow from nearly everyone in the village. However, he still doesn't seem to grow at all. Hue Boy's father is unable to help as he works away from home on a ship.

Sometimes Hue Boy liked to go to the harbour. There he watched the ships come and go and he could forget about his size.

One day a beautiful big ship came in. "Man, that looks good!" thought Hue Boy. "It's the biggest ship I ever saw!"

Then Hue Boy saw a very tall man among the passengers. The tall man walked straight towards him.

"Hello, Hue Boy," he said.

"Dad!" said Hue Boy.

His father took Hue Boy's hand and they walked away from the harbour and into the village. They walked past Miss Frangipani. They walked past Doctor Gamas and the wisest man in the village. They walked past Miss Harper and Carlos. And they walked past Hue Boy's friends from school. Then they met Gran and Mum.

And Hue Boy walked tall, with his head held high. He was the happiest boy in the village.

And then something happened to Hue Boy. He began to grow. At first he grew just a little bit. Then he grew a little more. Until the time came when his size didn't worry him anymore.

by Rita Phillips Mitchell
illustrated by Caroline Binch

Hue Boy

Display life-size figures of Hue Boy walking beside his father against a tropical background. Put feeling words for Hue Boy and his father around the figures.

Add photographs of each class member lined up and smiling with a central caption reading *We are all different and that's great.*

PSHE and citizenship learning objectives

◆ To think about ourselves and learn from experiences (1d).

◆ To understand belonging to various groups and communities, such as family (2f).

◆ To recognise some of the ways people look after each other (2g).

◆ To identify and respect the differences and similarities between people (4c).

◆ To acknowledge that family and friends should care for each other (4d).

◆ To feel positive about ourselves (5b).

Background notes

Rita Phillips Mitchell's story *Hue Boy* is set in a Caribbean village. It illustrates a different lifestyle and explores two key PSHE issues – the difficulties for Hue Boy of living without his father, who is obliged to work on ships and is thus away for long periods, and the vulnerability the boy feels because of his height, his 'difference' from the other boys in the village. Although this story is used in the Families chapter, the ideas suggested also focus upon the concept of respecting difference. In this story Hue Boy's difference is exaggerated because of the absence of his father. The absence of his main role model makes him more vulnerable.

Vocabulary

Father, small, tall, away, growing, worry, happy, walking tall.

Discussing the text

◆ Read the whole piece to the class then, read again the introduction to the text. Ask the children how Hue Boy felt and what troubled him.

◆ Ask the children why they think Hue Boy wanted to be tall. Did it really matter?

◆ Do the children know why Hue Boy's father was working away from home? How do they think Hue Boy's father would feel about having to work away from his family? What would he miss? What would Hue Boy and his mother miss when Hue Boy's father was away at sea? (Caution may be needed if children in the class are experiencing parental loss either through work, separation or bereavement.)

◆ Look at the passage when the ship comes in. Ask the children why Hue Boy liked to go to the harbour. How did he feel when he saw a big ship come in? Record their suggestions on a flip chart.

◆ Focus the children's attention on the description of Hue Boy's dad. Does this help explain why Hue Boy wanted to be tall?

◆ Ask the children how Hue Boy felt when he walked home through the village with his father. Why did it matter that he was seen by all the important people in the village?

◆ Discuss what special thing happened once Hue Boy's dad came home. What was the most important thing – that he grew taller or that his size didn't worry him any more?

PSHE and citizenship activities

◆ Choose a few confident children to stand at the front of the class. Ask the other children to look at their differences focusing on such things as height and hair colour. Point out that it would be really boring if we were all the same. Use a strip of identical figures cut out of paper. Contrast this with your models. Ask the children why it is useful to have people of different shapes and sizes. Illustrate this by asking the tallest child to get something from a high shelf. Ask the smallest person to squeeze through a small space, such as under your chair. Emphasise that it is good to be different.

◆ Draw around each child then ask them to paint their outlines with their own unique characteristics. Display these life-size figures.

◆ Tell the children they are going to draw a picture of themselves and a picture of another person who is different to them. Underneath have them record that *it is good to be different*. These pictures can form part of a display.

◆ Get each child to make a *Family Book* with a page for every member of their family (this can include their carers and extended family). Each page should have a profile of the person's name, age (this could simply state *grown-up* or *old*), what they look like, what the child likes about them and a picture of them.

◆ The children can role-play in pairs the scene where Hue Boy's father comes home, one child being Hue Boy, the other Hue Boy's father. Ask them to focus on what they would say to each other as they walked home. In small groups, get the children to work on a second scene of a homecoming of an important family member in their imagined family. What would they all say and do to celebrate?

◆ Ask the children to write a story about coming home from a holiday spent without their family. What did they miss? What would they say and do as soon as they got home?

Further literacy ideas

◆ Ask the children to write about what is special about their father (or other male member of their family, for example an uncle or granddad).

◆ Explore vocabulary linked to size including adjectives, for example *big, small, huge, tiny*; comparatives, for example *bigger* and *smaller*; and superlatives, for example *smallest* or *tallest*. The children could write them in appropriate calligrams, for example *tall* as a long thin word.

◆ Record on a flip chart places the children like to go, like Hue Boy going to the harbour. Why do they like their special place? What do they do there? Ask them to draw a picture of their special place with themselves in it.

◆ Look together for words in the text that finish in *all*. Record other words and add them to the class wordbank.

◆ Make a special place in the home corner. Surround it with the adjectives used in the activity above. Children can read or look at the story again in this special place.

◆ Investigate changing the onset in the word *small* keeping the rime *all*. How many new words can the children make?

◆ Look together in the text for titles of people such as *Doctor, Mr, Mrs, Gran, Mum*. How many other titles can the children think of? (Professor, Captain, King, Queen, Princess, Prime Minister, Headteacher.) Can they find any in other books?

◆ Read *Titch* by Pat Hutchins to the class and ask the children to suggest similarities in the theme of being small and finding this difficult.

Not Now, Bernard

Genre
narrative
fiction with
repetition

Introduction to the text

A little boy comes into the house to find his dad. He has something important to tell him.

"Hello, Dad," said Bernard.
"Not now, Bernard," said his father.

"Hello, Mum," said Bernard.
"Not now, Bernard," said his mother.

by David McKee

Not Now, Bernard

Create a two-column display. On the left-hand side have phrases such as *When I am ignored I feel...* Use speech bubbles, pictures and key feeling words. On the right-hand side list some of the strategies to use when being ignored (discussed below).

PSHE and citizenship learning objectives

- ◆ To recognise likes and dislikes, and what is fair and unfair (1a).
- ◆ To recognise choices can be made and the difference between right and wrong (2c).
- ◆ To understand rules for, and ways of, keeping safe (3g).
- ◆ To recognise how behaviour affects other people (4a).
- ◆ To recognise that family and friends should care for each other (4d).
- ◆ To take and share responsibility (5a).
- ◆ To consider social and moral dilemmas in everyday life (5g).
- ◆ To be able to ask for help (5h).

Background notes

Not Now, Bernard by David McKee is a black-comedy fantasy book familiar to both children and Key Stage 1 teachers. In this case the book's main storyline, of the monster eating Bernard, an event unseen by his busy parents, has been put to one side. Only the opening sequence has been kept to allow teachers to explore with the children the basic problem of being ignored. The activities focus upon the development of strategies for getting noticed without becoming aggressive or passive.

Vocabulary

Ignore, not now, hurt, unloved, frustrated, angry, patient, busy, right and wrong, safe.

Discussing the text

◆ Ask the children what Bernard's problem is. Have they ever had the same problem? Ask them to give examples and using key words, such as *ignore*, record the types of situations when children have been ignored.

◆ Explore how it makes the children feel when they are ignored (bad about themselves, that they don't matter and are not loved or cared about).

◆ Ask the children why Bernard's mum and dad didn't want to listen to him (focus on non-deliberate reasons, such as too busy, too preoccupied or worried, insufficient time).

◆ Discuss with the children what Bernard could do to get his parents' attention, or to make himself feel better. Could he dance up and down, touch his mother, take her hand, ask her to listen to him for

a moment? Alternatively, could he find a brother or sister, or a grandma or granddad, or a friend to tell this important thing to? Ask what they think would be the wrong thing for Bernard to do. Suggest running away, shouting, pushing or hitting. Do the children know why these things are wrong? (They hurt people or may put Bernard in danger.)

◆ Ask the children what they think will happen next in the story. Discuss possible alternative endings with them.

PSHE and citizenship activities

◆ Ask the children to draw a picture of Bernard looking angry and frustrated. Suggest they use a big speech bubble and write *I feel…*

◆ Tell the children that they are going to pretend to be Bernard's mum or dad and that they are to write a letter to Bernard telling him why they ignored him.

◆ Ask the children to act out a scene in groups of three, each child adopting the part of either Bernard, his mum or his dad, and taking the scene forward from the scenario in the text. Does Bernard try to get their attention or does he go away and feel miserable? If any group plays out the latter scenario show it to the class and ask the children what he could do to make himself feel better (telling his gran or granddad, or telling a friend, or writing down the message and handing it to his parents).

◆ Ask the children to talk in their groups about what would happen if Bernard did something wrong, for example running away, shouting or yelling, smashing something, or pulling his mum around and trying to hit her. Do they know why these things are wrong? What would be the consequences of this kind of behaviour? Would it help Bernard?

◆ Ask the children to think about a time when they have ignored their parents or teachers, such as when called to come down to breakfast, or to get up for school, to go to bed or tidy up. What did their parents or teachers do when their wishes were ignored? How do they think their parents or teachers felt about being ignored? Role-play a situation when this has happened. What should the children do to make things better after ignoring someone? (Apologise and act quickly next time.)

◆ Discuss the fact that sometimes people we love or who are important to us don't have time to listen. Reaffirm the strategies the children can use to help them, such as finding a better time when mum or dad are less busy, for example bathtime or bedtime; being patient; clearly asking for the person to listen and affirming that it is important, touching the person gently and looking at them; finding someone else to listen to them; writing it down and giving the note over to the person; or helping parents with some of their jobs around the house. Finally, point out to the children the importance of making sure they try not to ignore their parents, teachers and friends. Suggest they politely explain if they need to do something else first.

Further literacy ideas

◆ Ask the children to rewrite the story from Bernard's mum or dad's point of view. Suggest the use of either speech marks or a speech-bubble format, depending on the age group.

◆ Get the children to draw a picture to illustrate the text, concentrating on the facial expressions of all the characters.

◆ Suggest the children write a poem based on a similar situation as the text, focusing on using a repeated line, for example *'Not now, Joanna,' said her sister.*

◆ List rhyming strings for the words *not* and *now*. Write these on individual word cards for the children to sort into rhyming groups.

◆ Have another set of word cards ensuring that each word is duplicate. Make a game of pairs to develop spelling of high frequency consonant–vowel–consonant words.

◆ Focus at capital letters at the beginning of names. Get the children to write their own name with a decorated or illuminated enlarged first letter.

◆ Look at another text by David McKee such as *Elmer* (see the extract on page 74). Ask the children if there is anything similar about these two stories in terms of storyline or language, interest and enjoyment.

Genre
postcards

Postcards home

Introduction to the text
Suzanna is in Year 2 and she is going on a holiday with her class. They are going with their teacher Mr Hobbs, another teacher and some parents. They will be staying at a special hostel for schools and will be doing lots of exciting things by the seaside. Suzanna begged her mother to let her go when they had the letter, but now as she's waiting by the coach to get on board she's changing her mind. She is frightened and wants to go home. It is too late. Her mum, dad and big brother are waving her off, telling her she will enjoy it when she gets there. Suzanna isn't so sure.

Friday morning
Dear Mum and Dad and Tom,
*   I hate it here. I had a bad night. I had to sleep in a room with three other girls. They wouldn't let me have the top bunk. Come and get me soon.*
love Suzie

Saturday morning
Dear Mum and Dad and Tom,
*   It's cold and I don't like the food. Richard Fell is horrible. He pushed me on the sand and laughed when I shouted at him. I hate him. Mr Hobbs said it was an accident. It wasn't. Richard had to say sorry but he didn't mean it. Only two more days then I can come home.*
love Suzie

Sunday morning
Dear Mum and Dad and Tom,
*   Had a great time here yesterday. I was able to go on all the rides and I climbed up a tree and crossed a rope bridge. It was scary but I did it. Richard helped me. He's not as nasty as I thought. The girls let me go on the top bunk. We are taking turns. The food is okay. Mr Hobbs makes us laugh with his jokes.*
love Suzie

Monday morning
Dear Mum and Dad and Tom,
*   I cannot believe we have to go home tomorrow. I want to stay. So do the others. The trip to the castle was brill. We pretended we were attacking it. Richard was very funny. I led the attack. We won and got the castle. Can I come again next year? Can I bring Richard and Kate and Jane and Sally and Mr Hobbs to tea?*
Got to go,
Suzie

Postcards home

Display brochures of school residential holidays and holiday postcards.

PSHE and citizenship learning objectives

◆ To recognise likes and dislikes (1a).

◆ To take part in discussions with one other person and the whole class (2a).

◆ To understand belonging to various groups and communities, such as family, school and friendship groups (2f).

◆ To recognise rules for, and ways of, keeping safe (3g).

◆ To recognise that there are different types of teasing and bullying (4e).

◆ To feel positive about ourselves (5b).

◆ To develop relationships through work and play (5f).

◆ To be able to ask for help (5h).

Background notes

This will be a good text to use if the class is going on a residential holiday in Year 2 or will be going on one early in Key Stage 2.

Vocabulary

Holiday, unhappy, fun, teasing, feelings, frightened, camp.

Discussing the text

◆ Read the introductory text with the children. Ask why Suzanna isn't keen to go on her school holiday. Will her family be right about her enjoying herself? Have the children ever been about to go on holiday without their family and suddenly not wanted to go? Did they have a good time? Do they think Suzie will?

◆ Ask the children what sort of writing the text is (a type of letter called a postcard). Make sure they recognise a postcard, that they know it is sent usually when on holiday and that it tells other people about the holiday. Ask if they have sent postcards when on holiday themselves.

◆ Read the first postcard with the children. Who do they think Suzie is writing to? Suzie is very unhappy, why do the children think this is so? Is she missing her family? Is she missing her own bedroom? Is she tired? (Record the suggestions on a flip chart.) Will Suzie's mum come for her, do they think? If not, what might her mum do? (Telephone or write back.)

◆ Read the second postcard with the children. Is Suzie still unhappy? Write down the children's reasons why. Ask them to consider the incident with Richard. What do they think really happened? (Allow the children free range with their ideas, both with Richard being horrible and it being just fun or an accident.) Lead a discussion about what is teasing and 'fun' or 'rough and tumble', and what is bullying or nastiness. (The benchmark is the victim's feelings.) Point out that Suzie probably told Mr Hobbs about the push. Affirm that this is the right thing to do if they think someone is being nasty to them, or if they are hurt or upset. Why was Richard made to apologise and why is that important? Reiterate that when we've hurt someone, even if it is an accident, we should always say sorry.

◆ Read the third postcard. How does Suzie feel about her holiday now? Discuss with the children why Suzie has changed her mind about the holiday – raise issues about her getting used to the situation, being successful in the tasks and activities, feeling good about herself, realising that sometimes children are teasing rather than trying to be horrible and that she has a chance to get the top bunk because the girls in her room are being fair and taking turns. List on the flip chart, opposite the reasons for unhappiness, the reasons why she is now enjoying herself.

◆ Read the last postcard with the children. What are Suzie's feelings now? Why do they think she has changed her mind about the holiday? Look at the long list of people she wants to invite for tea. Why has she invited these people? Why does she now count Richard as a friend rather than someone she doesn't like?

◆ Discuss with the children what would have happened if Suzie had refused to go on the holiday, or her parents had collected her on the first day. Make the point that sometimes we need to persevere with something we don't like at first and then things get much better.

◆ Point out to the children that Suzie went on this holiday without her familiy, but she did go with her friends. Would Suzie have had such a good time if her family were with her? Encourage them to realise that they can have fun away from their adult family members on a holiday with their classmates.

PSHE and citizenship activities

◆ Ask the children to pretend to be Suzie and to express their feelings on first arriving at the hostel in a letter to their mum. What don't they like? Do they want to come home?

◆ Discuss with the children the kind of holidays schools organise for their pupils. Ask them to imagine the sort of things they would want to do with their schoolmates if they went on holiday with them. Remind the children that it would have to be cheap activities so that the holiday wouldn't cost too much and everyone could take part. Remind them also of safety considerations. How would they manage to please everyone? (By including a range of different sorts of activities.) Look at brochures for school residential holidays for ideas, then in pairs, ask the children to draw up a brochure advert showing their ideal school holiday, including where they would sleep, the activities they would do and the food they would eat.

◆ The children can draw a three- or four-frame cartoon version of the postcards showing Suzie's thoughts and feelings as she goes through the holiday. Tell them they should show a change from unhappiness to happiness.

◆ Encourage the children to learn their own address and telephone number off by heart.

Further literacy ideas

◆ Discuss the type of sentences and language used in a postcard with the children, pointing out the short, succinct and descriptive sentences. Look at typical themes, for example weather, places visited, how people are feeling and the informal signing off and opening words. Point out that they are written informally and don't have the sender's address on.

◆ Ask the children to imagine that the whole class have gone on holiday together without their families. Tell them they are going to write a postcard to a member of their family or a friend. Get them to think about using short, descriptive sentences on the identified themes and to write these on real pieces of card or blank postcards. Children could then colour a picture of their holiday on the front.

◆ Ask the children to write a postcard from a fairytale character, such as Goldilocks describing her visit to the Bears' house, or Jack to his mum about his visit to the Giant's castle.

◆ Design a class poster of a favourite holiday destination using the caption *Wish you were here*. Encourage them to use pictures and words for the poster showing the destination's special amenities.

◆ Discuss the use of commas to replace the connective *and*. Ask the children to form pairs. One child should write lists of things in a long sentence, such as a shopping list or things to take on holiday, then swap with their partner who rewrites their sentence using commas.

Dear Mummy

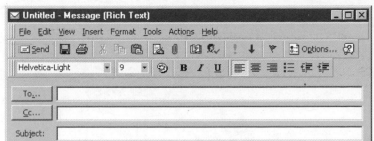

PHOTOCOPIABLE

Genre
fiction in
e-mail and
postcard
formats

Untitled - Message (Rich Text)

File Edit View Insert Format Tools Actions Help

Send | | | | | | | | | | | | | | | Options... |

Helvetica-Light | 9 | | B *I* U | | | | | | |

To...

Cc...

Subject:

Hi Mummy,

Dad has told me to e-mail. I have been very sad since you flew off to your army base in Cyprus. Dad says we might be able to come over later for a holiday. Can we? Sam is happy. Dad is looking after him. He fed him beans and chips last night and let him stay up. He doesn't understand that you will be away for a long time. I have put up a picture of you by his bed. I have one too.

I miss you,
love Katherine

Spring

Untitled - Message (Rich Text)

File Edit View Insert Format Tools Actions Help

Send | | | | | | | | | | | | | | | Options... |

Helvetica-Light | 9 | | B *I* U | | | | | | |

To...

Cc...

Subject:

Hi Katherine,

I miss you too, and Sammy and Daddy. It is lovely here. The sun is shining and I have been swimming in the sea. We will sort out the holiday for the autumn. I am busy at work. We are in classes, like you, learning lots of new things. Work hard in school. I have a picture in my locker of you all and I kiss you goodnight when I go to bed. Give Daddy and Sammy a hug from me,
love Mummy

Untitled - Message (Rich Text)

File Edit View Insert Format Tools Actions H

Send | | | | | | | |

Helvetica-Light | 9 | | B *I*

To...

Cc...

Subject:

Hi Mummy,

Dad says we can telephone you on your birthday night. Be ready at 6pm. Sammy had an accident at nursery today. He fell off the climbing frame. He hurt his leg and arm and has big bandages on them. Daddy says 'it looks worse than it is'. He was given a bar of chocolate to make him feel better. I did a good picture today. Daddy helped me scan it in. I am sending it to you. It is a picture of us together on holiday in Cyprus. Daddy says it's dinner time, got to go,
love Katherine

Summer

Untitled - Message (Rich Text)

Insert Format Tools Actions Help

| | | | | | | | | | | | Options... |

| 9 | | B *I* U | | | | | | |

To...

Cc...

Subject:

Hello Katherine,

The picture is terrific. I have it up in my locker. We are out and about on exercises, putting those things we learned into practice. I'm sorry that Sammy was hurt. Tell Sammy to be more careful on the climbing frame. Enjoy the summer holiday.
love Mummy

Autumn

Dear Auntie Sharon,
    Cyprus is great. It is warm
and the seawater is so clean I
can see the stones underneath.
Mummy is suntanned. She is
coming home at Christmas.
love Katherine

Auntie Sharon
11 Pine Grove
Stratford-upon-Avon
Warwickshire
CV4 8MU
England

ARRIVALS

Winter

ARMY

Dear Mummy

Create two parallel displays with a timeline showing seasons and months in the middle. The top display shows three scenes from Katherine's life, each scene prepared by one group of children. The bottom display shows three scenes showing her mummy's life during the same period, each picture to be prepared by one group. The last two pictures can break the timeline and show the holiday and then the reunion at Christmas.

PSHE and citizenship learning objectives

◆ To realise that people have needs and there are responsibilities to meet them (2e).
◆ To recognise that family and friends should care for each other (4d).
◆ To understand that sometimes close family members cannot be with us all the time and to develop strategies for supporting each other when someone is away.
◆ To recognise that keeping in contact with people who are away is very important.

Background notes

Sometimes children are obliged to cope with periods when one or other of their parents are working away from home. Keeping up contact with the absent parent is really important to sustain the relationship. This set of e-mails emphasises the positive aspects of managing this absence. The absent parent has been chosen to deliberately challenge the usual stereotype of the father working away whilst the mother tends the child or children.

Vocabulary

Away, missing, e-mail, mobile, postcard, coming home.

Discussing the text

◆ Read the first e-mail exchange with the class. Ask the children to think of words to describe how Katherine feels. Record these words under the sub-heading *Katherine* on a flip chart. Why does her mother have to stay away from home? How would her mother be feeling? Record on the flip chart under the sub-heading *Mum*. Discuss why Katherine is writing to her mother. Is it important that Katherine writes? Why?

◆ Ask the children how Katherine helps Sammy to remember his mum and not feel so sad. How does Dad help his children to feel less sad?

◆ Read the next e-mail exchange. Ask the children what sorts of things Katherine writes about to her mother. Are they important things or just about everyday things that happen to Katherine and Sam? Ask the children what they think Katherine's mum would have felt when she received the summer e-mail from Katherine. Record these suggestions on the flip chart. Ask if they think Katherine's mum is missing home and her family. What sort of things would she be missing? (Birthdays, doing things together, seeing them every day, sharing the good times and helping out when things are difficult, having meals together, having fun.)

◆ Ask the children why Katherine wanted to telephone her mother. Do they think it is better to telephone than e-mail? Ask them to give their reasons.

◆ Katherine and her family get to stay in Cyprus for a holiday because her mum works out there. Make the point that sometimes having a parent working away means they can visit exciting places.

◆ Ask the children to imagine the moment when Katherine's mum comes home. What would Katherine do or say when her mum got back to the house? What would she show her mum? How would they spend time together?

◆ Discuss with the children how Katherine and her family would manage without their mum. How would they help each other to stay cheerful and cope? Some children may be able to contribute from personal experience. Sensitivity will be needed in these situations.

PSHE and citizenship activities

◆ Ask the children to imagine themselves as a sister or brother of Katherine. Ask them to write a letter to 'Mum' to tell her about Katherine and how she is and what she is doing. Tell them they can finish the letter by saying what they want to their 'mum'.

◆ In pairs, get the children to pretend that one of their best friends has to go away with their parents to America. Together they can write a letter telling their friend about what is happening in school and in their home lives to make the friend feel that they are still sharing a friendship. Tell them they should remember to include the ordinary things, not just the special events, such as describing the weather and what's on TV. If any child has left the class they could be written to as a class exercise. This could also be done for any child who is absent due to long-term sickness.

◆ In groups of four, get the children to make a play using puppets or teddies where one member of a toy family has to go away for a short while. How will their characters help one another to feel better? (Encourage the expression of genuine feelings and consoling strategies in the plays.)

◆ Make a collection of the children's own family photographs, identifying the people in the photos and who they are in relation to the child.

◆ Make a timeline display using the following pictures (see display ideas). Take a scene from the story and in groups make a collage picture showing Katherine in or outside her house. The scene should reflect the time of year and the things mentioned in the text. The same group should make a corresponding picture of Katherine's mum showing what she was doing at each point in the year. Use these for the display. Two further pictures can be produced that bridge the timeline, one of the holiday, one of the homecoming.

◆ As a class, look up where Cyprus is in an atlas. Give pairs of children brochures for Cyprus to find out what sort of place it is. They could then make posters advertising a holiday there.

Further literacy ideas

◆ Get the children to illustrate the sequence of the story in cartoon format showing either or both points of view.

◆ A four-frame blank strip could be given to the children to draw and sequence pictures illustrating the four seasons. The children should add the correct season name to each picture and learn these.

◆ Look at examples of e-mail with the class. Identify the conventions of e-mail writing, particularly beginnings and endings. Compare these with the postcard and more formal styles of letter writing.

◆ Ask the children to write about their homes or bedrooms to a pen friend abroad.

◆ Form an Internet connection with a parallel class in another country or in another part of the country. Individual children can partner each other and send and receive e-mail messages about school and the work being done.

◆ Work with older children to set up a school website. Details of the work being done at that time could be described and illustrations scanned in, or programmed in using digital cameras.

◆ Children, in pairs, could e-mail their parents at work or at home, or the teacher, where appropriate, with a message about what they are doing in class.

Osa's Pride

Genre
*narrative
fiction with a
different
cultural
setting*

Introduction to text

This is a story about Osa who is a seven-year-old girl living in a village in Africa. She lives with her mother and brothers on her grandmother's coffee farm. Her father has gone away to fight a war and has not come back. Because Osa is stubborn she won't believe that her father is not coming back. She makes up stories about him being a hero and rich, and that he will come back for her and take her to the city.

Now at first, they listened and agreed: but when I spoke only of *my* father and forgot to listen to *their* stories, about *their* parents they soon began to leave me alone. I made believe I did not care and let them know that when *I* grew up I would go away from this little village and be educated at the University in the big city, and – just like my papa – *I might decide never to come back, either!*

My Gran'ma let me be for a while watching me carry my pride about, listening to nobody, head in the air. But Uncle Doma, seeing me playing all alone, came over and crouched down to ask me,

"Where are all your friends, Osa?"

"I don't need them!" I sniffed.

Uncle Domo shook his head.

Just then, Gran'ma called me over to her side.

by Ann Grifalconi

Osa's Pride

Display models and pictures of Osa and her family.

PSHE and citizenship learning objectives

◆ To recognise what is right and wrong (1a).

◆ To recognise choices can be made (2c).

◆ To recognise that people have needs and that there are responsibilities towards meeting these (2e).

◆ To recognise how behaviour affects other people (4a).

◆ To recognise that families and friends should care for one another (4d).

Background notes

This story deals with the problem of acceptance of loss in families. Osa refuses to accept her father's death and instead retreats into making up heroic stories and adventures. She ignores her friends and ends up without anyone.

Vocabulary

Dead, father, friends, stories, stubborn, pride, listening.

Discussing the text

◆ Discuss Osa's family situation together, who she lived with and why her father was not around. Make sure the children understand that Osa's father is probably dead. Ask them why they think that Osa was so unhappy. (Because she didn't want to believe that her father wouldn't be coming back.) Was Osa right to refuse to believe people when they said her father wouldn't be coming back? (Allow the children to express their own opinions on this.)

◆ Discuss with the class what Osa did next and why (made up stories about her father). Ask the children if they think that was right or wrong. (Again the answer can be either – look for their justifications for their reasoning. Osa could have been right. She wasn't necessarily lying.)

◆ Osa did do something wrong though, when she was with her friends. Ask the children to find the passage in the text that tells them about this (she failed to listen to her friends when they wanted to talk about their own fathers and family). Ask the children what the outcome of that mistake by Osa was (her friends left her and wouldn't play with her).

◆ Discuss with the children how Osa felt when her friends went away (there are clues in the last section of the text). Ask confident individuals to come out and act out these feelings – sadness, anger, pretending not to care about anyone, loneliness.

◆ Osa suffered from stubbornness. Ask the children what they think this means. Can they give some example of times when they have been stubborn themselves (such as refusing to eat any dinner because they couldn't have exactly what they wanted, taking the football away from their friends because they couldn't be captain)? Why is this behaviour wrong? (It upsets friends and family and doesn't get them what they want.)

◆ Ask the children what they think will happen next in the story. Will the story end happily or will Osa grow up and leave her village forever? Record possible ideas on a flip chart.

PSHE and citizenship activities

◆ The children can write an ending to the story with a happy outcome using the ideas discussed in the last discussion activity.

◆ The children can draw a picture of Osa with a huge thought bubble in which is shown a picture of her heroic soldier father. Underneath the picture ask the children to write *Osa wants her father to be…*

◆ In groups, the children can make a model of Osa's home with figures for Osa's family and Osa in the middle of her family. Stress that Osa was not alone, she is surrounded by people who love her.

◆ Using a large piece of paper divided vertically down the middle, the children, in pairs (possibly friendship pairs), can paint a dual-image picture. On the left, one of the pair should paint a picture of Osa when she is at her most unhappy, painting the background with colours that match Osa's feelings. On the right of the paper, the other child can paint a picture of Osa at the end of the story when she is feeling happier. The background colours can reflect that feeling too. This works best on an easel, but if done simultaneously needs to concentrate on cooperation and organisation to prevent pairs irritating each other.

◆ Ask the children to imagine that they are a special friend of Osa's. What can they do to help her? Get them to work out a little play in pairs to show their ideas.

Further literacy ideas

◆ Using Osa's name as a starting point, look at vowels and consonants with the children.

◆ Select children to read aloud parts of the text, asking them to focus on observation of sentence structure and expression. Draw their attention to the words in italic and the exclamation marks, and make sure they read these with emphasis.

◆ Play a pass-the-pebble game in a group or whole-class situation. Children pass a pebble or special object around and when they have the pebble they must say a word that rhymes with the word previously given. Begin by giving an example yourself from the text, such as *war/door*, *father/rather*, *pride/hide*, *friends/lends*.

◆ Look together at similes for *stubborn*, *pride* and other words, for example *as proud as a lion* or *peacock*, or *as stubborn as a mule*. Ask the children to look for other similes from the animal family.

◆ Ask the children to write about why their family is so important to them.

◆ Ask the children to write about who they live with and who makes up their families.

◆ Get each child to draw an outline of their mother (or other significant female) and then write about her inside the outline.

◆ Ask the children to write a list of instructions about how to be a good friend. Ensure that commas are used correctly to separate items.

Friendship

One of the greatest gifts and pleasures of attending school is the formation of long-standing friendships. Thus, friendship is one of the key concepts to be explored with children of all ages. In the infant classroom, friendships often form as a result of children sitting together on the same table or working together in a common literacy or numeracy group. Children begin to meet peers from a whole range of backgrounds and upbringings, and these friendships allow for mixing and visiting, collective fun and a testing of their own assumptions in a broader society. It fuels the process of learning if children can decentre, a psychological growth that will form the basis of adult relationships.

Friendship also brings conflict and hurt and many fallings out. It can be a test of dominance and morality. It can also be a cruel selection process based on physical attractiveness and material wealth. It requires the development of compromise, moral judgement, non-violent conflict resolution, loyalty and constancy.

Helping children to cope with the dynamics of friendship is the inevitable lot of the class teacher, as is testified by the oft-repeated phrases *he won't let me play with him* and *they won't let me be friends*. Thus, this area provides rich fodder for the Literacy Hour, and the likelihood of active engagement from the children. There are countless texts that deal with this theme. These are just a few.

We are friends

Genre
*poem with
repetition*

When you are sad – I make you happy,
When you are in trouble – I help,
When you want to talk – I listen,
And when you want to play – I play too.

We are friends.

When I am cross – you tell me a joke,
When I have no sweets – you share yours with me,
When I run – you run too,
And when I tell you a secret – it is kept.

We are friends.

by Gillian Goddard

We are friends

Display two life-size figures holding hands. Around the figures are the matching pairs of phrases from the poem and the children's own phrases.

PSHE and citizenship learning objectives

◆ To think about ourselves and learn from experiences (1d).

◆ To realise that people have needs and that there are responsibilities to meet them (2e).

◆ To recognise how behaviour affects other people (4a).

◆ To know that friends should care for each other (4d).

◆ To develop relationships with other children or friends (5f).

Vocabulary

Friends, listen, help, share.

Discussing the text

◆ Read the first verse with the class. Discuss what the writer of the poem does to be a good friend. Ask the children what sort of things they do for their friends. Record their ideas on a flip chart.

◆ Ask the children which part of the poem tells them that this is a poem about two friends.

◆ Read the second verse with the class. What is the poet saying here? How do the children's friends help them? Record their thoughts on the flip chart.

◆ Create extra verses or lines together using the children's ideas. Use the intervening *We are friends* line between each verse.

◆ Direct the children's attention to the structure of the poem. How many lines are there in each verse? Do the verses share some words? Why do they think there is a dash between the phrases? How else could they write this? (A comma, or a full stop.)

PSHE and citizenship activities

◆ Divide a strip of paper into four. Invite individual children to draw a picture in one of the sections to illustrate the two friends together as described in a line in the poem. This will translate it into cartoon format. Half the class can take one verse, the other half can take the second. The illustrations will reinforce the concepts shown in the poem, that there is mutual help offered in friendship.

◆ Discuss with the children, in a group or as a whole class, words that describe a good friend. Record these on the flip chart. Add to these other descriptive words that are the opposite of good-friend characteristics, for example *hates, ignores, spoils, selfish*. Use this collective mixed list for children to select and sort. Give the children a sheet of paper each with a circle drawn on it labelled *A good friend is…* Each child can select from the collective list and copy the words into the circle. This then provides an assessment of each child's understanding of the friendship words and their ability to read the words with meaning.

◆ Ask the children to match the pairs of words from the poem together in terms of need and response, for example *sad/happy, talk/listen, trouble/help, no sweets/share*. This reinforces the knowledge of the right response to the need.

◆ Ask the children to role-play in pairs a scene from the poem. Discuss the things that could be making them sad, for example a lost or broken toy. How would a friend make them happy? Perform this for the class and for an assembly on *friends*.

◆ Show a picture of a child 'caring' for another child and ask the children, in pairs, to write a caption for the picture.

Further literacy ideas

◆ Children can write their own couple of lines with the words *When I… – You…* given to them.

◆ Look at the phrase *We are friends*. Together find some two-, three- or four-letter words that can be made from the letters, for example *as, in, if, end, far, send, ran*.

◆ Using the role-play ideas, ask the children to draw comic-strip pictures in pairs, and to add to these speech bubbles inserting appropriate statements, such as *I am sad, I am cheering you up*.

◆ Look together at antonyms linked to friendships, for example *sad /happy, talking/listening*, then extend this to general ones. Put the words onto cards to make an opposites snap game. The children can play this with an adult or friends.

Old Bear

Genre
fiction by a
significant
author

Introduction to the text

Bramwell Brown has a feeling that today is going to be a special day and then suddenly remembers a long lost friend. Long ago Old Bear was put away in the attic for safe keeping. Bramwell Brown and the other toys, Rabbit, Duck and Little Bear, then stage a daring rescue to retrieve him from his forgotten place using a toy aeroplane.

Little Bear jumped up and down with excitement. "Old Bear! Old Bear! I've found Old Bear!" he shouted.
"So you have," said Old Bear.

"Have you been lonely?" asked Little Bear.

"Quite lonely," said Old Bear. "But I've been asleep a lot of the time."

"Well," said Little Bear kindly, "would you like to come back to the playroom with us now?"

"That would be lovely," replied Old Bear. "But how will we get down?"

"Don't worry about that," said Little Bear, "Bramwell has thought of everything. He's given us these handkerchiefs to use as parachutes."

* * *

That night, when all the animals were tucked up in bed, Bramwell thought about the day's adventures and looked at the others.

Rabbit was dreaming exciting dreams about bouncing as high as an aeroplane.

Duck was dreaming that he could really fly and was rescuing bears from all sorts of high places.

Little Bear was dreaming of all the interesting things he had seen in the attic, and Old Bear was dreaming about the good times he would have now he was back with his friends.

"I *knew* it was going to be a special day," said Bramwell Brown to himself.

by Jane Hissey

Old Bear

Display a large picture of the five friends in bed together with the caption *Friends are…* using key words given by the children.

PSHE and citizenship learning objectives

◆ To think about ourselves and learn from experiences (1d).

◆ To know how to set simple goals, for example to be kind to someone who looks lonely (1e).

◆ To recognise choices can be made, and recognise the difference between right and wrong (2c).

◆ To realise that people have needs, and that there are responsibilities to meet them (2e).

◆ To understand about belonging to various groups, such as friends (2f).

◆ To contribute to the life of the class and the school by being a good friend (2h).

◆ To recognise that behaviour affects other people (4a).

◆ To know that family and friends should care for each other (4d).

◆ To develop relationships through work and play (5f).

Vocabulary

Friends, rescue, sorry, risk, feelings, lonely.

Discussing the text

◆ Read the introduction with or to the children. Ask them who they think Bramwell Brown is. Record possible ideas on a flip chart, for example *a boy, another toy.* Ask the children why Old Bear was put up in the attic. Direct them to the name of the bear for a clue about this if they are unsure. Do they have toys that have to be kept safe out of their way or out of the way of younger brothers and sisters? Why is that a problem? (They can't play with the toy, or they sometimes forget it is their toy.)

◆ Look at the introduction again and ask the children how these friends managed to rescue Old Bear from the attic (they flew up in a toy plane). Did just one toy do the rescuing or were all the friends involved in the rescue? Was it dangerous to fly up so high, do they think? Should the friends have risked such a dangerous rescue attempt? (Allow a range of responses here but stress the purpose of the rescue was to be reunited with an old friend.)

◆ Read the first section of the text together. How do the children think Old Bear has been feeling up there in the dusty dark attic? Ask them to find the words in the text that tell them. Would he have missed his friends? Ask the children to imagine that they were Old Bear. How would they feel? Might they have been angry or sulky when Little Bear arrived? Explain that sometimes when friends remember us and come to ask us to play we are angry with them for forgetting us in the first place and we don't want to play.

◆ Ask the children why Old Bear was lonely. What does being lonely mean? Have they had times when they felt lonely? What helped them to feel better? (Finding someone to talk to or play with.) What should we do if we find someone who looks lonely or sad? (Ask them to play with us or talk to them.)

◆ Read the last part of the text together. Ask the children what all the toy friends were dreaming about. Why was that? Who do they think was the most pleased about what happened and why? Why was it such a special day for Bramwell?

PSHE and citizenship activities

◆ Ask the children if they have days that they feel are going to be special, days when something exciting is going to happen. In pairs, get them to try to work out a story where something exciting happens to make the day special. Write a story beginning *The day was the same as any other day, but I knew it was going to be special because…* Alternatively, ask the children in pairs to act out a short scene based on their ideas and show the others.

◆ Ask the children to tell one another about their special toys, then to draw a picture of the toy and either write or talk about why this toy is so special. Discuss with the children what makes a toy special. Point out that it is usually one that they can love, or that they can share with others.

◆ Ask the children to label an outline of a child with words that describe what makes a good friend. Collect some more words and copy these onto a big picture of Old Bear and his friends.

◆ Individual children can create a picture that shows Old Bear in the centre with lines linking to pictures of his four friends (Rabbit, Duck, Bramwell and Little Bear). Under each linked figure ask them to write *I like Duck because he is…* Children could repeat this activity with a picture of themselves and their friends. (If there are children without friends you may wish to omit this extension activity.)

◆ Talk to the children about what stops people being friends. What makes friends fall out? Ask the children to think about playground situations or not sharing and list their ideas on a flip chart, for example *not sharing, not letting others play, getting cross, someone wanting their own way all the time, breaking friends if someone doesn't do what they want, saying unkind things.* Ask pairs of children to act out a short scene showing the suggested scenarios. After each scene ask children to tell the two actors what they think they should have done. Children can replay the scene if they wish with the correct strategy in place, or just confirm the right strategy.

◆ Ask the children to form a circle and hold hands. Either sing a song together or do a circle dance to stress the togetherness point. Children could contribute lines to a song about friends using a well-known nursery rhyme or popular tune, for example:

> Friends are caring,
> Friends are strong,
> Friends forgive one another
> And friends admit they are wrong.

Further literacy ideas

◆ As a class, write an instructional text about how to be a good friend.

◆ Ask the children to write about a good friend that they have, describing why their friend is a good friend. (Be sensitive to children who may not have any friends. In this instance, ask all children to write as if they were one of the characters in the text and say what is special about one of their friends.)

◆ The children can write a poem entitled 'Good friend – bad friend' with alternate verses about what it is like to be a good friend and a bad friend.

◆ Encourage the children to bring their favourite toys into school and share orally why their toy is special. Develop this into a shared-writing activity. Choose one child's contribution to use as a focal point for everyone to write about that toy.

◆ Look together at descriptive names, such as *Old Bear, Little Bear.* Ask the children for an example to describe themselves, such as *Lovely Suzie.* They can be funny but they must be positive not negative about themselves, so not *Bad Bob* or *Naughty Joanne.* Some children may need help. This could be developed into alliterative names for themselves, such as *Sunny Surjit* or *Lovely Luke.*

Little Beaver and The Echo

Genre
fiction with predictable and patterned language

Introduction to the text

Little Beaver lives all by himself by the side of a pond and is lonely. One day he hears his echo and thinks it's someone else who is all alone and needs a friend. So he sets out to find him. While crossing the lake Little Beaver meets a duck, an otter and a turtle who are also looking for friends. Finally, he finds a wise old beaver…

"It was the Echo," said the wise old beaver.

"Where does he live?" asked Little Beaver.

"On the other side of the pond," said the wise old beaver. "No matter where you are, the Echo is always across the pond from you."

"Why is he crying?" said Little Beaver.

"When you are sad, the Echo is sad," said the wise old beaver. "When you are happy, the Echo is happy too."

"But how can I find him and be his friend?" asked Little Beaver. "He doesn't have any friends, and neither do I."

"Except for me," said the duck.

"And me," said the otter.

"And me," said the turtle.

Little Beaver looked surprised. "Yes," he said, "I have lots of friends now!"

And he was so happy that he said it again, very loudly: "I have lots of friends now!"

From across the pond, a voice answered him: "I have lots of friends now!"

by Amy MacDonald
illustrated by Sarah Fox-Davis

Little Beaver and The Echo

Display a scene of the lakeside with Little Beaver and his friends playing, thought bubbles coming from their heads. A thought bubble repeating the friends' thoughts is coming from the far side of the lake.

PSHE and citizenship learning objectives

◆ To think about ourselves and learn from experiences (1d).

◆ To recognise choices can be made (2c).

◆ To realise that people have needs and understand the responsibility to meet them (2e).

◆ To understand about belonging to various groups (2f).

◆ To contribute to the life of the class and school (2h).

◆ To know how to make simple choices to improve well-being (3a).

◆ To recognise how behaviour affects other people (4a).

◆ To know that friends should care for each other (4d).

◆ To develop relationships in work and play (5f).

Vocabulary

Echo, lonely, beaver, friends.

Discussing the text

◆ Read the first sentence of the introduction with the children. Ask them why they think Little Beaver was lonely. What does it feel like to be lonely? Record the children's answers on a flip chart.

◆ Read the rest of the introduction. Ask the children if they think they know what an echo is. Could they give a voice example? Where do echoes come from? (Tunnels, caves, big halls and buildings, sometimes in the countryside where there are big hills or rocks.)

◆ What happened when Little Beaver thought there was a lonely person on the far side of the lake? (He went across the lake to look for the upset and lonely person who was crying.) Would the children do this, or would they stay where they are and feel miserable? Explain that sometimes we have to make an effort to find friends, even though we feel sad and miserable.

◆ Can the children tell you what Little Beaver found on the lake? (Lots of other animals who were lonely and needed a friend.)

◆ Read the remainder of the text with the class. What did the wise old beaver say when Little Beaver asked him about the friend he couldn't find? Do the children know what *wise* means?

◆ What did Little Beaver find out in the end? (That he had lots of friends.) Do the children think he understood what an echo was? (No.)

◆ Ask the children to tell you how Little Beaver felt when he realised he had lots of new friends.

◆ Can the children explain what happened to Little Beaver's 'echo' friend?

◆ What words in the introduction and text show how Little Beaver was feeling? Ask the children to underline these, such as *lonely*, *needs a friend*, *sad*, *happy*.

◆ Discuss with the children what Little Beaver did that led to him finding friends. (He went in search of the lonely person on the far side of the lake.) Remind them that if he had stayed where he was and stayed miserable, he wouldn't have found any friends.

PSHE and citizenship activities

◆ Ask the children if they have ever experienced a time when they have felt lonely because they had no friends. How did it feel? Record their words on the flip chart. Ask them to write a poem about loneliness using some of the words and to finish with a final verse where the lonely person finds a friend.

◆ Discuss what the children can do if they feel lonely and have no friends. Like Little Beaver they could go and find someone who looks sad and lonely too, or they could find someone to play with. They could start playing a game on their own, such as playing with a ball, or drawing. Other children might get interested, and they might feel better for doing something. They could also ask an adult they know and trust, such as a midday supervisor, a teacher, Mum or Dad, Grandma or the child minder, to help them find a friend. Ask the children to write a list of possible ways to find a friend or help themselves feel less lonely.

◆ Do the children think they would know if someone was lonely or without a friend? (They sit or stand alone and look miserable.) In pairs, ask the children to come up with a list of good ways of helping someone who looks lonely and who has not got a friend. (This should include allowing the lonely child to play with them.)

◆ Get the children to draw a picture of Little Beaver with his new friends. They can fill in thought bubbles for the otter, duck, turtle and Little Beaver.

◆ Set up a 'buddy' system in the class. Buddies look out for children who are lonely and without friends, and make friends with them and get them to play with other children. Discuss with the children that actually there are times when we just want to be on our own for a little while. Ask them how they could find out if someone wanted to be alone or wanted to really play?

Further literacy ideas

◆ Look together for the vowel digraph *ea* and find some words in the text with this combination. Using dictionaries and wordbanks, ask the children to find as many words with this blend as possible. Then help them to sort words into different-sounding *ea* lists, for example *feather, each*. Also investigate how the *ea* sound in *beaver* can be made with other graphemes.

◆ Get the children to rewrite the story from the point of view of the duck.

◆ Look up the meaning of the word *echo* together. Ask the children to look in information books for an explanation of what an echo is. To help this understanding of an echo take them under a local bridge or underpass if you have one.

◆ Investigate wise proverbs, such as *look before you leap*, that the wise old beaver may have said. Children could ask at home for family sayings with special meanings.

◆ Investigate calligrams with the children. Use echo as an example and then think of other words that could be written in this way, for example *shout* and *drip*.

School break

Genre
poetry

throwing grass
handstands

running
chasing
laugh

pass the ball
daisychains
tag me as you pass

sunshine
rain-pool splashing

hop
with arms
spread wide

smell of hawthorn
blossom

best friend
by my side

lie down
sunray spreading

wind on face
in hair

short time
warm time
fun share

joke
and cry
and care

by Joan Poulson

School break

Display the central words *We are friends,* surrounded by a circle of figures representing the class. Put up the words describing how to be friendly, the lists of ways of being a good friend and the pictures of friends playing from the previous activities.

PSHE and citizenship learning objectives

◆ To think about ourselves and learn from experiences (1d).
◆ To realise that people have needs and there is a responsibility to meet these (2e).
◆ To be able to contribute to the life of the class and school (2h).
◆ To recognise how behaviour affects other people (4a).
◆ To know that family and friends should care for each other (4d).
◆ To develop relationships through work and play (5f).
◆ To ask for help when it is needed (5h).

Background notes

Although this poem is about break-time in the playground, it provides a valuable context for the discussion about friend-based activities in this most powerful of situations for children. Having friends or not matters fiercely during playtime. It is a place too, where friendships are made, tested and broken with alarming frequency.

    The poem is simple and creates an alternative poetic form to that of rhyming couplets.

Vocabulary

Friends, play, lonely, best friend, loyal, trustworthy.

Discussing the text

◆ Read the whole poem with the children twice, first slowly and then more fluently. Ask the children what the poem is describing. Ask them individually to identify the lines they like best and if possible to explain why they like them.
◆ Draw attention to the middle lines *best friend, by my side.* Ask the children to look through the poem and underline the lines that demonstrate things friends do together at playtime, such as *chasing, running, laugh, pass the ball, tag me if you pass, fun share, joke and cry and care.*
◆ Discuss with the children the types of things they do with their friends in the playground. Record examples of the positive things on a flip chart. Make the point that playtime is more fun with friends to play and share the time with.
◆ Look closely at the last four lines *fun share, joke, and cry and care.* Ask the children if this is what they think good friends do together. Are there any words there that surprise them? (Cry?) What did the poet mean by this? If their friend is very upset or unhappy, do we sometimes feel like crying too? How can they suggest they help a sad friend feel better? (Tell a joke, play a game with them, give them a hug, listen to them, keep them company if they don't want to play, give them a sweet, let them play with a toy or game, tell the teacher that their friend is very sad.)
◆ Discuss with the children the times when they fall out with our friends, or when they don't have any friends. Ask them how it feels to have no one to play with at break time. Record these feelings alongside the friendship activities already listed on the flip chart. Ask the children how they can help

someone who has no friends and is feeling this way. (Go and ask them to join in their game.)

◆ Ask the children why they fall out with their friends. Sometimes it is their friend's fault, sometimes it is their fault – they won't share, they want their own way in the game, they are jealous of the fun their friends are having with other children. If they fall out with their friends what can they do? (Say sorry and join in again, forgive them and find someone else to play with for a while.)

◆ What do the children think makes a best friend? (Someone they like to spend a lot of time with, who is easy to talk to and fun to be with, who lives near and can play outside school hours, who likes the same things that we do, who is loyal, trustworthy and kind.)

P SHE and citizenship activities

◆ Ask the children to draw a picture of themselves with their best friend playing in the playground. Beneath the picture they can write *My best friend and I…* and list the things they do together.

◆ Can the children write a poem about what it is like to have no friends in the style of the poet? Ask them to conclude the poem with a final verse where they find a friend to play with.

◆ In groups, get the children to find some games that can be played in the playground with more than one person, like the tag game mentioned in the poem. Ask each group to choose their favourite game and show the others in the class how to play it. Make a class book of the games.

◆ Get the children to act out scenes in small groups where friends fall out and each go off in a huff. How do they become friends again?

◆ Suggest that the children make a card saying what they like about their best friend and give it to them.

◆ In small groups, get the children to make a list of the ways they can be a friend to someone in the playground. They can word-process the list and print off a copy for each person in the group.

◆ Ask the children to write a story about a friend they had who was not loyal and went off to play with others, leaving them alone. How did they feel? What did they do?

◆ Discuss with the class the difference between being a friend and being friendly. Suggest that although they can't always be friends with each other the whole class should be friendly to one another. How can they be friendly? Give some examples to get the children started. Ask them to paint their favourite words describing a way to be friendly and use these for a display, for example *being kind, smiling, helping, looking out for, letting them join in, sharing things, talking to them, listening.*

Further literacy ideas

◆ Choose a story or poem from the class library that is about being a friend. Read it to the class or, alternatively, ask a competent reader to.

◆ Contrast this type of poem with a rhyming poem. Ask the children which they prefer and why. Ask them to write a poem about friends choosing one style or the other.

◆ Children can write a riddle that describes their best friend in the class and other children can try to guess who it is.

◆ Look at the odd way we spell *friend*. It has a silent letter in it. Can anyone tell you which one it is? Do the children know any other words that have silent letters in them? (*Whether, gnome, gnat, write.*)

◆ Using the word *friend*, find as many words from it as you can, for example *fin, fir, end, fend, den, fire.*

Promises

Genre
poem with repetition

Introduction to the text
Sometimes friendships draw forth promises or pledges. This poem explores this idea and begins to raise the question of what is and is not a sensible and valuable promise.

I promise to be your friend for ever.
I promise to play with you every playtime.
I promise to share my sweets with you.
I promise to lend you my crayons if you need them.

I promise to wear the same colour clothes as you.
I promise to jump up and down every time I see you.
I promise to give you a million pounds.
I promise to buy you the biggest car in the world.

by Gillian Goddard

Promises

Display a list of promises or pledges from the class and from a range of organisations, such as Rainbows or Beavers.

PSHE and citizenship learning objectives

◆ To think about ourselves and learn from experiences (1d).
◆ To be able to contribute to the life of the class and school (2h).
◆ To recognise how behaviour affects other people (4a).
◆ To develop relationships through work and play (5f).

Vocabulary

Promises, pledges, vows, trust.

Discussing the text

◆ Discuss with the children what a *promise* is. (A statement that says that they will do something for someone.) Ask if any of them have made promises to their friends or family. (Don't ask them for the content of these promises.)

◆ Read the first set of promises from the text. Can the children think of any other examples of promises that a friend could make? Write these down on a flip chart.

◆ Discuss how important it is to keep promises. Do the children think it is very important or not so important? Why? (Allow a range of responses but stress that the reason we make promises is because it makes friendships much stronger.) Explain that later, if they marry when they grow up, they will be making very special promises to stay together and look after one another. These are called vows. Tell them that people make promises all through their lives and are expected to keep them.

◆ Ask the children how they would feel if someone promised to play with them and then didn't. What words would describe their feelings? (*Hurt, angry, miserable, wouldn't trust them again.*)

◆ Read the second set of promises from the text. Do the children think these are sensible promises? Consider sensible and silly promises together. Ask the children for examples of sensible promises, starting with the text examples and expanding them. Do the same for silly promises. Why are they silly? Are they achievable? Do the children think they will help make someone be a good friend? Stress the point that material gifts don't make for good friends; caring, sharing, listening and playing together do.

PSHE and citizenship activities

◆ As a class, look at other vows, pledges or promises. Look at the marriage ceremony words and those of the Beavers and Rainbows. In pairs, ask the children to choose their favourite pledge and say why they chose it and which part of the pledge is the most important.

◆ Ask the children to think about the kinds of promises they would want to make to their friends. Then, individually, get them to write these down and choose the most important one. Suggest they make a card that has this promise on it and give it to their friends.

◆ Discuss what promises could be made by the class to the class. Look at the rules of the class for ideas. Compile some class promises as a whole class. Word-process these and display them. The children can collectively say the pledge.

◆ Can the children think of a promise that you could make to them? Once a few are generated, steered towards the sensible, choose one and formally pledge to do that.

Further literacy ideas

◆ The children can write a series of promises that could be made to their family. Suggest they begin each sentence with *I promise to…*

◆ Invite the children to write a story about a time when they have broken a promise. Ask them to describe what happened and how they felt.

◆ Make up a nonsense poem about silly promises together.

◆ Find out about different words that mean *promise* by looking the word up in the dictionary and thesaurus, then making a wordbank of these words.

◆ Get the children to cut up the promises in the text and sort them into silly promises and sensible promises. They could also add some of their own.

◆ Ask the children to turn the sentences from the text into requests, for example *Will you promise to…?* Point out the use of question marks.

Respecting differences

When children are first born they see the world only from their point of view. As they grow up they begin to have contact with a wider range of people and experience a greater variety of situations— they need to develop an ability to see the world from other people's points of view as well as their own. Although some children will have attended a local or school nursery before they enter primary school, for others school will be their first real experience of having to play, work and share with other people who may not have the same beliefs, likes, abilities and attitudes as them. Young children tend to believe that everyone is exactly like themselves, looks like them, has feelings like they do, likes to do the same things. As children mature they do become aware of individual differences and preferences but do not always see these in a positive way.

This chapter will help you to move the children towards developing a respect for individual differences and preferences. It will encourage them to see that it is very positive that we all have different likes and dislikes, that we like doing different things, have different feelings and react in different ways to situations, and that in this way the world is made a much more interesting place. Discussion is encouraged within the whole class, small groups and in pairs to enable children to examine their own and others' viewpoints. The chosen texts focus on issues such as people's characters, physical looks, physical abilities, likes and dislikes. They also consider fair and unfair treatment of people linked to individual differences and encourage children to accept and respect these differences.

Depending on the age of the children within your class you will need to consider what other issues the texts may raise. Many issues are included in the discussion and activities, and you may be aware of specific individuals and situations within your class that will need sensitive handling, for example children with a disability or those who are a different race from the majority of other children in the school.

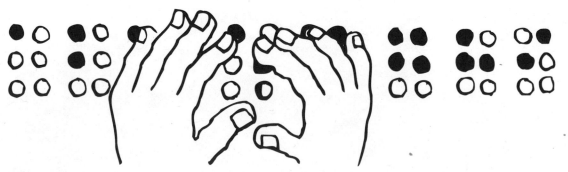

Michael

Genre
story with a
familiar
setting

Michael was different.
His teachers said…
he was the worst boy in the school.
He was always late…
and he was a little scruffy.
He was often cheeky.
And he never did what he was told, either.
"That boy will come to no good," his teachers said.
But Michael didn't listen.

by Tony Bradman
illustrated by Tony Ross

Michael

Display pictures of the children's drawings of Michael and themselves, with lists of antonyms and *ff* consonant clusters.

PSHE and citizenship learning objectives

◆ To recognise likes and dislikes, what is fair and unfair, and what is right and wrong (1a).
◆ To think about ourselves, learn from experiences and recognise what we are good at (1d).
◆ To recognise how behaviour affects other people (4a).
◆ To identify and respect the differences and similarities between people (4c).
◆ To feel positive about ourselves (5b).

Vocabulary

Characteristics, different, same, cheeky, scruffy, late, bad.

Discussing the text

◆ Read the text to the children. Cover up all the story except the first line and discuss what might be meant by *different*. What sorts of things do they think Michael will do? At home? At school?
◆ Show lines two and three and ask the children what they think the teachers in Michael's school might say about him. What might the worst boy in school do or behave like?
◆ Discuss lines four and five together. Question the children about whether being late and sometimes a little scruffy is bad. Which of them has been late? Which of them is sometimes a little scruffy? Assure the children that we all do these things at times.
◆ Focus on line six with the children. Ask them what being cheeky means. What do they think about children being cheeky? Is that worse than being scruffy or late? Discuss how behaviour can have an impact on others. Being late and scruffy may not be good, but they don't have an adverse effect on other people (although being late can be unfair on others). Being cheeky, however, can upset people and show lack of respect for them.
◆ Finish by reading the final three lines. Discuss with the children why Michael may have acted in this way. What do the children think may happen to Michael as he grows up and goes through the school? (He could become even naughtier and not have many friends or get excluded. Alternatively, he could grow up and become more sensible.)
◆ Share with the children the ending of the story – that Michael designs a rocket and flies into space and the teachers all say they knew he would go far! Does this change the children's image of Michael? (Explain to them that we all have good qualities and the potential to be successful – it is just a matter of finding these skills.) What do the children think about the teachers wanting to take credit for Michael's success when they hadn't really helped him?!
◆ What do the children think is meant by *different* in this particular story?

PSHE and citizenship activities

◆ Discuss with the children how each of them is different, for example in what they like doing at school. Point out that some of them love maths and some of them do not, some like reading and others do not, but it is good that everyone is different or the world would be a very boring place! Stress the point that difference is good.

◆ Make a graph to show the children's favourite and least favourite subjects. Use this to illustrate the above activity.

◆ Discuss with the children what they would like to be when they grow up and to write a paragraph about this. Their ideas can be shared as a wall display and the variety of ideas celebrated. Discuss with the children how each job needs different skills and point out that we need different people who possess different skills so that all the jobs get done. Stress that no matter what they choose to do, others should respect their choice.

◆ Invite a variety of visitors into school to discuss their jobs with the children, for example a nurse, doctor, vicar, police officer, another teacher, headteacher, secretary, cook, midday supervisor, firefighter, and so on. Investigate with the children the similarities and differences between the jobs (for example, some are active, some are quiet desk jobs and others involve helping people).

◆ Get the children to collect and display a variety of non-fiction texts, using class, school and local libraries, which look at people's jobs.

◆ Make a class frieze that has a self-painted portrait of every child on it. Display in the classroom, corridor or cloakroom with simple sentences, such as *I am… I like…*

◆ Ask the children to work in pairs and discuss with each other what they like doing, for example playing or reading. Can they work out how they are the same as each other and how they are different? In pairs, get them to make a chart showing their similarities and differences.

◆ Ask the children to write about themselves in the third person and in the style of the text, for example: *Jane was different. Her teachers said… She was the best girl in the school…*

◆ In a circle-time or similar activity, discuss with the children how they feel when a member of the class is being disruptive, misbehaving, or being naughty. Why do they think children do this? (Suggest they are sad or frustrated by their work.) Are the children sad themselves, cross, or frustrated by work that is too hard or too easy? Do they think that disruptive children realise the effect they have on other children's feelings and actual learning? What class rules can they write to help children respect each other's feelings when they are playing and working?

Further literacy ideas

◆ Focus on the character of Michael and ask the children to find and list the words which describe his character in the text.

◆ Using the words found in the text, ask the children to draw a picture of Michael.

◆ Ask the children to write a list of words to describe their own character, these can then be developed to produce sentences which describe themselves. These sentences can be displayed as a *Guess who we are?* activity, or made into lift-the-flap books that the children can share.

◆ Ask the children to create antonyms linked to words describing Michael's characteristics, for example *late/early, different/same, scruffy/tidy.* The children can make their own list of opposites linked to their own or Michael's characteristics.

◆ The children can rewrite the sentences from the text using antonyms, for example, *Michael was ordinary…*

◆ Get the children to write a school report about Michael. Give them subject headings to scaffold their writing.

◆ Ask the children to write a letter home to Michael's parents reporting on his behaviour. Look at the conventions of letter layout, and how to begin and end formal letters (this would be a good opportunity for using a word-processing template).

◆ Ask the children to write an entry for Michael's diary about how he feels he is treated at school.

◆ Look at words with the consonant clusters *ff* within them, for example *scruffy, different,* and so on.

Elmer

Genre
story by a significant children's author

> **Introduction to the text**
> Elmer is a member of an elephant herd which has elephants of all ages and sizes. They are all grey except for Elmer, who is multi-coloured. He makes all the other elephants happy with his jokes. But then one night Elmer becomes tired of being different and decides to do something about it. He covers himself in juice from some elephant-coloured berries turning himself into a grey elephant. None of the other elephants notice him when he gets back to the herd.

The elephants were standing absolutely still: Elmer had never seen them so serious before. The more he looked at the serious, silent, still, standing elephants, the more he wanted to laugh. Finally, he could bear it no longer. He lifted his trunk and at the top of his voice shouted:

"BOOO!"

The elephants jumped and fell all ways in surprise. "Oh my gosh and golly!" they said and then saw Elmer helpless with laughter.

"Elmer," they said. "It must be Elmer." Then the other elephants laughed too as they had never laughed before.

As they laughed the rain cloud burst and when the rain fell on Elmer his patchwork started to show again. The elephants still laughed as Elmer was washed back to normal. "Oh Elmer," gasped an old elephant. "You've played some good jokes but this has been the biggest laugh of all. It didn't take you long to show your true colours."

"We must celebrate this day every year," said another. "This will be Elmer's day. All the elephants must decorate themselves and Elmer will decorate himself elephant colour."

by David McKee

Elmer

Display a copy of the book with a replica of an elephant and one of Elmer (these are available to buy or you could make one).

PSHE and citizenship learning objectives

◆ To think about ourselves, learn from experiences and recognise what we are good at (1d).

◆ To take part in a simple debate about topical issues (2b).

◆ To recognise that people and other living things have needs, and that there are responsibilities to meet them (2e).

◆ To understand about belonging to various groups and communities, such as family and school (2f).

◆ To recognise how behaviour affects other people (4a).

◆ To identify and respect the differences and similarities between people (4c).

◆ To recognise that family and friends should care for each other (4d).

◆ To recognise that individual differences make us very special and that we each have special skills or qualities.

Vocabulary

Special, different, sad, upset, celebrate, elephant, grey, multi-coloured.

Discussing the text

◆ Read the introduction to the text. Discuss with the children where elephants live and what an elephant looks like. Ask who has seen an elephant on TV, in a book or at the zoo. Ask why they think Elmer is different.

◆ Read the extract with the children all the way through. Then ask the children how they think Elmer must have been feeling as he tried to get to sleep the night he decided to change his colour (he felt different from everyone else and that he wanted to be the same as the other elephants). Why do they think he had these feelings? What might have happened to him that day to make him feel this way? Why did Elmer want to look like the other elephants?

◆ How do the children think Elmer felt after he had changed his colour? (That he was now the same colour as all the other elephants and so no longer stood out as being different. He felt the same.) How did the other elephants react to him? (They didn't notice him because he was grey but they actually really missed him because he was so special because of his lovely colours and this made them sad.)

◆ At the end of the story the elephants decided to have a special celebration each year to remember Elmer – ask the children what this reminds them of. What special celebrations do they have each year to celebrate individual specialness? (For example, birthdays, Christmas, saints' days.)

◆ Explain to the children that sometimes we want to be the same as everybody else, but that it is much better to be different and special. Ask the children about the things they feel they have to have that are the same as everybody else's, for example trainers, toys, hairslides. Do they think it makes them any better or happier to have the same things as other people? Make the point that the people who lead fashion, rather than copying it, are different from everyone else.

PSHE and citizenship activities

◆ Discuss with the children how Elmer was a very special elephant but he didn't know he was until this event in the story happened. Talk about special people in the school and how what they do every day helps us, even though they may not realise they are special, for example midday supervisors, school secretary, caretaker, headteacher. The children, in pairs, can write to one of the people in school who helps them every day, thanking them, explaining why they are special and how they make daily life easier and better. Make a collection of class cards for special people, such as Mother's Day or birthday cards. Get the children to design a card for someone special, such as a midday supervisor, their father, granny, childminder or crossing patrol. They can make and send the card with a suitable greeting inside. This can be done on the computer, importing a picture, painting a design or creating headings.

◆ The children could write about someone who makes their day brighter. It could be an adult or another child in the school.

◆ Get the children to draw or paint their own Elmer with bright colours and patterns. What will he look like? Cut out each elephant and make a display of all the elephants celebrating together on Elmer day. If you have a copy of the book show the children the picture at the end. This will remind them that each and every one of us is different and special.

◆ Involve every child in making a large painting of Elmer and make sure everyone colours in one of his squares. Display this with words upon it describing what makes people special, for example *being helpful*, *funny*, *kind*, *caring*, *thoughtful*.

◆ The children can choose a way to help others for a day and make a badge to stick on themselves explaining how they will do this. Emphasise that it could be something very simple, such as *I will smile all day to cheer people up*. Praise all the children for trying at the end of the day. In this way the children are encouraged to think about how their actions affect others and how they can make being in their class a more pleasant experience.

Further literacy ideas

◆ Provide the children with an *I am special* certificate. Identify with each child one special skill, ability, or characteristic to write on their certificate and use it as a handwriting practice exercise.

◆ Focus the children on the use of prepositions by getting them to describe the location of a square on Elmer (for example, *My square is below a black square, above a white square, next to a green square*). This work could be displayed with a picture of Elmer and other children could try and find the squares.

◆ Ask the children to make an illustrated book retelling the story from Elmer's point of view.

◆ More able children can use a thesaurus to find alternative words for the characteristics of nomintated classmates, for example, *nice – lovely*, *pleasant*, *fine*.

◆ Make a collection of non-fiction books containing information or pictures of elephants. Develop the children's use of the specific features of non-fiction texts (index, contents and pictures), by focused questioning and activity setting. For example, ask the children to make a list of questions and to find the answers themselves or to ask other class members to find the answers.

◆ With the children, make a list of questions which they would like to find the answers to about elephants. They can write out their questions and display them as a web. The non-fiction collection of books can be used to find their answers. These can be written as simple non-chronological reports (support this writing with scaffolded worksheets for the less able), which can be used to make a class book about elephants.

◆ Get the children to draw and label a diagram of an elephant, naming the parts of the body correctly.

Goldilocks and the three bears

Genre
traditional
story

Once upon a time, as you may recall, there lived a little girl called Goldilocks. Goldilocks was an inquisitive child who liked to go off on adventures all on her own. Now on this particular sunny summer's day Goldilocks wandered into the woods behind her house to play. Before long she came upon a small cottage and guess what she did?

Yes, you guessed, she crept inside.

Now, as you already know, this cottage belonged to three bears, a mummy bear, a daddy bear and a baby bear, and you are going to tell me they had popped out for a walk while their porridge cooled.

So we find Goldilocks inside the house exploring. When the three bears returned all was not as they had left it! The porridge bowls on the table each had a spoon in and someone had obviously been hungry.

"WHO'S BEEN EATING MY PORRIDGE?" growled Daddy Bear.

"WHO'S BEEN EATING MY PORRIDGE?" gasped Mummy Bear.

"WHO'S BEEN EATING MY PORRIDGE AND EATEN IT ALL UP?" cried Baby Bear.

The three bears looked around the room, but there seemed to be no one hiding. Suddenly Daddy Bear noticed his chair had been moved and his newspaper knocked off the arm.

"WHO'S BEEN SITTING IN MY CHAIR?" growled Daddy Bear.
Mummy Bear looked and saw her chair had porridge spilled all over it.

"WHO'S BEEN SITTING IN MY CHAIR?" she gasped.

"WHO'S BEEN SITTING IN MY CHAIR AND BROKEN IT ALL TO BITS?" cried Baby Bear.

The three bears were not at all happy about the state of their little cottage. Suddenly, from upstairs, they heard a loud yawn. Quietly they crept up the stairs to find where the noise was coming from. Daddy Bear, followed by Mummy Bear, followed by Baby Bear holding onto Mummy Bear's hand. Slowly Daddy Bear opened the door to the bedroom. He saw a rumpled unmade bed.

"WHO'S BEEN SLEEPING IN MY BED?" He hissed.

"WHO'S BEEN SLEEPING IN MY BED?" Mummy Bear gasped.

Baby Bear's eyes nearly popped out of his head as he cried,
"WHO'S BEEN SLEEPING IN MY BED AND IS STILL THERE?"

I bet you know how the story ended, don't you!

Retold by Jackie Barbera

Goldilocks and the three bears

Display a collection of different versions of the story. It is helpful if children are familiar with the traditional version of the text.

PSHE and citizenship learning objectives

◆ To recognise what they like and dislike, what is fair and unfair, and what is right and wrong (1a).
◆ To take part in a simple debate about topical issues (2b).
◆ To recognise choices can be made (2c).
◆ To agree and follow rules for the group and classroom, and understand how rules help (2d).
◆ To understand about belonging to various groups and communities, such as family and school (2f).
◆ To recognise how behaviour affects other people (4a).
◆ To take and share responsibility (5a).
◆ To consider social and moral dilemmas in everyday life (5g).

Background notes

Many traditional tales provide plenty of opportunity for discussing right and wrong. In the story of Goldilocks and the three bears the idea of right and wrong can be taken further to consider how Goldilocks did not respect other people's property, belongings or feelings. She appears to have happily explored the bear's cottage without thinking once about how they would feel when they found their porridge gone, their chairs broken and their beds slept in. This tale can be used to help children think about respecting each other's belongings, personal space and feelings.

Vocabulary

Feelings, broken, unfair, naughty, thoughtless, belongings, possessions.

Discussing the text

◆ Read the text to the children without giving them the title and ask which story the extract is from. What sort of story is this? (Traditional.) Do they know any other traditional tales? Have they heard other versions of this story?

◆ Using the extract consider with the children what the three bears expected to find when they arrived back from their walk in the woods and what they actually did find.

◆ What do the children think Daddy Bear thought when he looked at the table and saw his empty bowl? How did Mummy Bear and Baby Bear feel? (Worried about the fact that someone had been in their house, or cross that someone had eaten their breakfast because they were hungry.)

◆ What do the children think the bears felt when they saw their chairs and beds? How would the feelings of the bears develop as they realised more of their things had been taken, damaged or used? (They would probably have become angrier and upset that someone had damaged their things.)

◆ What do the children think Goldilocks did when she woke up and saw the bears? Many of them will remember from hearing the story previously, but they may have heard different versions so discuss this.

◆ What do the children think Goldilocks should have done on finding the house? What would they do themselves?

PSHE and citizenship activities

◆ In pairs, ask the children to discuss whether they think Goldilocks is a naughty girl or not, and to report their opinion back to the class justifying why they think this.

◆ Ask the children to share examples of times when they have felt upset, disappointed or hurt by things other people have done to their belongings.

◆ Discuss with the class how we should treat the possessions of other people. Are there any school or class rules that relate to this specifically?

◆ Talk with the children about respecting other people's belongings and feelings. Look at the school or class rules and discuss why each rule is there (look especially at the rules regarding property). If you do not have rules, then as a class, write a set. If you do have some, consider whether they are clear, fair and whether they are regularly kept. The children may be able to suggest some changes.

◆ Take in a special possession of your own to show the children. Try to choose something that may seem insignificant to them so that you can explain that it has emotional value attached to it. Ask the children to write about a special possession of their own and what makes it special to them. Make these into a class book and then read the book together. Discuss the fact that what is considered special by them need not be expensive or worth a lot of money, or be special to anyone else. Stress that because of this it is very important that we respect other people's belongings, even if they do not appear to have any value.

◆ Draw a class picture of one of the bears and surround it with feeling words based on finding the damage Goldilocks had done (such as *sad*, *cross*, *worried*, *upset*).

Further literacy ideas

◆ Look together at the use of the capitalisation in the speech of the bears. Why do the children think these words are a different size? (To illustrate their relative strengths and tones of voice.)

◆ Look with the children at the use of speech marks to demarcate the spoken text. Ask each child to choose a section of the story to illustrate and use speech bubbles to show what each bear is saying. Each speech bubble can use appropriate-sized writing for the bear who is speaking.

◆ Make a collection of different versions of the story. Look with the class at whether it has been written in the same way. Ask the children to decide which version they like best based on plot, language, illustrations and so on. Make a display showing the different endings, making different groups responsible for a particular ending illustration.

◆ Get the children to re-enact the story in role-play, or using props and dressing-up clothes.

◆ The children could write their own set of rules for the class, for example for a particular use of equipment, use of the role-play area, how to behave at wet playtime. These can be laminated and displayed in an appropriate place.

◆ Ask the children to retell the story – focusing on plot, using captions, pictures and arrows to record the main events. Use these to make a class book or wall display. Older children could retell their own modern-day version or change the things that Goldilocks did in the traditional version (she could visit the house of a pop group and use their hair-styling products and make-up).

◆ Write a class letter of apology to the three bears from Goldilocks.

◆ Ask the children to write a newspaper report about the crime. Make a collection of reports from a local newspaper and look at the layout, headlines and the way a report is written. Provide less able children with a report frame to fill in.

◆ As a class make a *Wanted* poster for Goldilocks, explaining what she has done wrong.

Louis Braille

Genre
recount and
information
texts

Text 1

My name is Louis Braille. I was born
in a small French town a long time
ago in the year 1809. One day, when
I was four years old, I was playing in
my father's workshop and I had a
terrible accident with a sharp tool
which hurt my eye and eventually I
became blind. In order to go to school I
had to live away from home in the city of Paris. I lived in a
special school for blind people where I learned to look after
myself. It was here at the school that I invented Braille to help
myself and my friends learn to read and with the help of a
Braille machine we could at last write.

When I grew up, I became a teacher at the school and helped
my children to read and write using Braille.

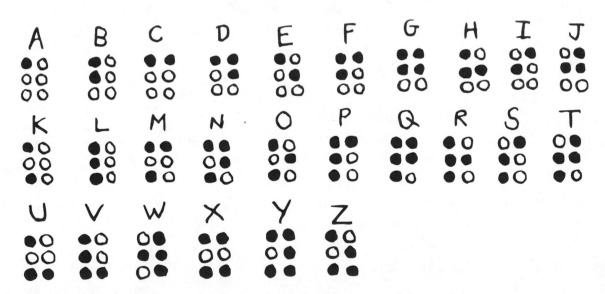

Text 2

Braille is a special alphabet to help blind people read. It is
named after the man who invented it, Louis Braille. It is written
on a machine called a Brailler that is like a typewriter. The
Brailler punches dots, which you can feel, onto paper. Each
letter of the alphabet has a different pattern of dots as shown in
the picture. Blind people then feel these dots and work out what
the words say.

Louis Braille

Make a display about sight, including Braille messages for the children to read. They won't be able to feel these but if done in bold pen they can decode the words. An NLS training video *Special Needs in the Literacy Hour* (available free of charge to schools) shows a boy using a Braille machine in school and would be useful for the children to see.

PSHE and citizenship learning objectives

◆ To realise that people and other living things have needs, and that they have responsibilities to meet them (2e).

◆ To understand the process of growing from young to old and how people's needs change (3d).

◆ To identify and respect the differences and similarities between people (4c).

◆ To be able to meet and talk with people (5e).

Background notes

Louis Braille was born on 4 January 1809 in Coupvray, a small French town near Paris. He was blinded in one eye in an accident whilst helping his father, a shoemaker. This damaged his eye, which became infected, and this infection spread to his other eye, leaving him blind by the time he was four. Louis eventually became a teacher but although he had developed his own system of reading, and most importantly the only system of writing for the blind, it was not a system that was used in his lifetime. He died on 6 January 1852 from tuberculosis.

However, today Braille is recognised worldwide and is used for virtually every language and in nearly every country.

Vocabulary

Sight, eyes, infection, Braille, non-fiction, reading, print.

Discussing the text

◆ Read the text with the children and establish that this is a real story about a little boy who lived nearly 200 years ago.

◆ Discuss with the children what being blind means and how this would affect their lives. Do any of the children know anyone who is blind or finds it hard to see? (Be sensitive to any children in the class who may have a visual impairment. It is important that the discussion is not about feeling sorry for people, but about differences and how these are dealt with.) Discuss how other senses are often improved to compensate.

◆ Emphasise to the children that nowadays there would probably be something the doctors could do to cure the infection in Louis' eyes without risking infecting their own eyes. But also discuss how we do have to look after our eyes and protect them when we are doing things that may cause accidents.

◆ Talk with the children about what we use our eyes for every day.

◆ Explain to the children about Braille and how it is used. Use the illustration of the Braille alphabet to focus on how someone would read Braille. Discuss how it is still used today. Explain to them that computers can print Braille and that many blind people have Braille keyboards so that they can use a computer.

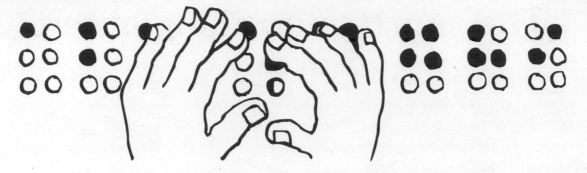

◆ Talk about how important it is for everyone to be able to read, but also how important writing is in our lives to record what we do, what we know, to explain things, and so on. What does being able to read allow the children to do? (Think about daily activities that involve reading, like going shopping or reading instructions.) Ask the children to suggest their own examples and make the point that they can read and enjoy lots of lovely stories and poems, and find out about things by reading from books and at the computer. Point out that we often write things down to help us remember things like dates or shopping. Discuss how Braille has made all of these things possible for a blind person to do.

PSHE and citizenship activities

◆ Consider with the children how special their eyesight is and make a list of things they use their eyes for.

◆ Write to the Royal National Institute for the Blind asking for information about how blind people are supported. Do they have any local visiting speakers who could talk to the children? Visit the RNIB website (www.rnib.org.uk/braille/braille.htm) which will enable the children to type something and translate it into Braille, as well as downloading a Braille typeface.

◆ Visit The Guide Dogs for the Blind Association website (http://www.guidedogs.org.uk) for information about how funds are raised and dogs are trained. It is also possible to arrange school visits by puppy walkers and guide dog owners to talk to the children about the work of the trainers and dogs (telephone 0870 600 23 23). Consider ways the class could take part in fund-raising for a charity for the blind.

◆ Invite an optician into school to talk about their job, or if your school is close to an optician's arrange to take the class on a visit.

◆ Make an optician's shop role-play area. Involve the children in designing and resourcing it based on the information from the optician's talk or visit.

◆ Look at other types of leisure activities that don't require sight. For example, make a garden where the emphasis is on scent rather than foliage and flowers, or explore things in the classroom using touch.

Further literacy ideas

◆ Ask the children to write a poem about what they see with their eyes.

◆ The children can write their names in Braille dots, and these could be displayed as part of a general display about sight or put on the children's trays. Older children could use tapestry needles to make the dots and try to read each other's by touch.

◆ Make labels and signs for the optician's role-play area.

◆ Make a class book about eyes and how to look after them. Gather information from books, visitors, nurses, opticians or the Internet. Make a glossary for the class book explaining the terms used and also an index.

The tenth good thing about Barney

Genre
narrative
fiction

Barney was brave, I said.
And smart and funny and clean.
Also cuddly and handsome, and he only once
ate a bird.
It was sweet, I said, to hear him purr in my ear.
And sometimes he slept on my tummy and kept
it warm.

Those are all good things, said my mother,
but I still just count nine.

Yes, I said, but now I have another.

Barney is in the ground and he's helping to
grow flowers.
You know, I said, that's a pretty nice job for
a cat.

by Judith Viorst

The tenth good thing about Barney

Display pictures, photos and poems about cats.

PSHE and citizenship learning objectives

◆ To think about ourselves, learn from experiences and recognise what we are good at (1d).

◆ To know about the process of growing from young to old (3d).

◆ To recognise that family and friends should care for each another (4d).

◆ To take and share responsibilities by looking after pets well (5a).

◆ To feel positive about themselves (5b).

Background notes

This text looks at the characteristics of one child's pet cat. The child is asked to think of ten good things about Barney, the cat, in order to help him or her cope with their feelings after Barney has died. However, the child can only think of nine. Eventually he or she thinks of the tenth thing by highlighting the fact that each pet is different and has their own special attributes. Links can be made here with people's characteristics and how each of us is special and different.

This text also considers how we each deal with emotions differently and that when sad things happen some of us cry, some of us get angry and some of us go very quiet. How we each react depends on our characteristics and children should be helped to see that just because other people don't react as they do it doesn't mean they do not have similar feelings.

Vocabulary

Brave, purring, smart, handsome, cuddly, characteristics, special.

Discussing the text

◆ Begin by reading the first paragraph and conceal the second half of the text from *Those are all good things*. Ask the children who they think Barney is. Ask them to give evidence from the text to support their answers (such as *cuddly, purr, slept on my tummy*).

◆ Revisit Barney's strengths and characteristics in the text, and discuss with the children how they think each relates to a cat. Record the characteristics on a flip chart and form them into a web diagram.

◆ Look at the second half of the text with the children. What do they think has happened to Barney? How does the text make them feel? How did the child in the story feel about this? What did the child think to cheer him or herself up a bit?

PSHE and citizenship activities

◆ Choose a person everyone in the class knows, such as a story character or a famous person (a pop star or footballer), and make a web diagram of that person's characteristics. Discuss whether we all think the same way about people.

◆ Get individual children to make a web diagram of their own characteristics. Focus on the words that describe these, for example *kind*, *funny*, *grumpy*.

◆ Discuss the feelings that the second half of the text evokes. The children can make a list of things that make them happy and sad. Discuss with individual children strategies for coping with the sad things.

◆ Ask the children to write a poem about a pet they have had, or would have liked to have, describing what is special about the animal.

◆ Make a graph to show how many pets there are in the class and what children have what pets. Use this as a lead into discussing how pets should be cared for.

◆ Get the children to write a set of instructions for looking after a pet. For those who don't have a pet get them to find out how to look after a cat, bird or fish. Make these into a class book.

◆ Make a class pet shop or vet's role-play area. Involve the children in making posters about looking after pets properly.

◆ Talk with the children about how they have felt when a pet or relative has died. How did they show these feelings? You could share your own personal experiences with the children and talk about how different people behave in different ways when they are sad and upset. Point out that some are quiet, some cry, some get cross.

Further literacy ideas

◆ Make a collection of character descriptions to look at as a class or in a group. Use some of the characters from other texts you have read as a class, such as *Michael* on page 71.

◆ In pairs, ask the children to make up a character web for a fictitious character and to develop these into a short description. The collection of texts gathered in the activity above will help them in the composition of this.

◆ Ask the children to make a timeline of what has happened to them each year of their lives so far. What do they think may happen next? (Move into the next class, have a birthday, have a new sibling, move house.)

Amazing Grace

Genre
narrative fiction from a range of cultures

Introduction to the text

Grace is a little girl who loves listening to stories and then playing and acting out all the tales she has heard at home and at school. She particularly likes acting out exciting parts. One day at school her teacher tells the class that they are going to perform the play of Peter Pan. Grace is very excited and can't wait to get one of the parts.

"You can't be called Peter," said Raj. "That's a boy's name." But Grace kept her hand up.

"You can't be Peter Pan," whispered Natalie. "He wasn't black." But Grace kept her hand up.

"All right," said the teacher. "Lots of you want to be Peter Pan, so we'll have to have auditions. We'll choose the parts next Monday."

by Mary Hoffman
illustrated by Caroline Binch

Amazing Grace

Display a copy of the book if you have one.

PSHE and citizenship learning objectives

◆ To recognise what is fair and unfair, and what is right and wrong (1a).

◆ To understand about belonging to various groups and communities, such as family and school (2f).

◆ To recognise how behaviour affects other people (4a).

◆ To identify and respect the differences and similarities between people (4c).

◆ To feel positive about ourselves (5b).

Background notes

The story ends happily and Grace deservedly gets the part of Peter Pan because she is the best actor in the class. The best person for the job is chosen irrespective of gender or colour.

Vocabulary

Audition, play, feelings, hurt, pantomime, story, characters.

Discussing the text

◆ Ask the children to recall what Grace really liked doing. Why do they think she liked listening to stories? Talk about what makes a story – character(s), setting, a beginning, middle and end, and so on. Relate this to stories read recently in the class.

◆ Grace loved to act out stories. Ask the children about stories they act out. What stories are they? How do they act them out? Do they play on their own or with others?

◆ Discuss with the children the concept of a play. Explain to them what the class in the story were going to do and explain what an audition is.

◆ Revisit the text and get the children to identify which part Grace wanted.

◆ Discuss with them the reasons Raj and Natalie used to tell Grace she could not be Peter Pan. What do the children think about these reasons? (Some children may have been to a pantomime where the leading boy is usually played by a girl and the leading older lady perhaps by a man, so discuss this with them.) Discuss also the issue of the colour of Grace's skin and how this is not important. Explain that it is only Grace's acting ability that needs to be considered.

◆ Ask the children to suggest ways that people should be auditioned. Lead them towards talking about how the selection should be based on the best actor for the role.

◆ Discuss how Grace would feel about Raj and Natalie's comments (upset because the comments were aimed at characteristics which she cannot change). Have the children ever felt like Grace did? (For example, any girls that have not been allowed to play football at playtime.)

◆ Make a list with the children of skills the person playing Peter Pan would need to have – a strong voice, be able to learn lines, able to pretend to be someone else, and so on.

PSHE and citizenship activities

◆ Ask the children to imagine that they are Grace and to write or talk about how they felt when Raj and Natalie, who seem to be her friends, made the comments about her not being able to be Peter Pan. Why do they think Raj and Natalie might have made these comments?

◆ Use role-play for the children to explore ways that Grace could have responded to Raj and Natalie. Encourage the children to have a polite but assertive response.

◆ Make a collection of stories (fiction and non-fiction) that show a variety of heroes or heroines from a variety of cultures. Point out that not all heroes are white males as projected by many texts, there are also female and different-race heroes, for example Mulan.

◆ Discuss how Grace may have reacted to the comments made by the other children (she could have withdrawn, not played with the others, gone home, been sad or become more determined to succeed). What do the children think she did? What would they have done? Share with the children the ending of the story, the fact that it made Grace more determined and at the audition she got the part she wanted because she was the best. Ask them to write about things that have happened to them that have made them feel sad or not included. How did they react?

◆ Discuss with the children how we often say things without thinking about how it will make other people feel. Can they think of occasions when they have fallen out with a friend due to a misunderstanding? Do they think Raj and Natalie really thought about Grace's feelings? Do the children think they meant to upset her?

◆ Ask the children to make a list of rules about how to treat other people.

Further literacy ideas

◆ Make a tally chart to show the children's favourite stories. Using the information from this, ask the children to make a graph and display both with copies of the books. Discuss which are the most popular and the least popular and why. Is there a particular genre that is most favoured? Explain to the children how everyone likes different things in a book.

◆ Ask each child to write about their favourite story and why they particularly like it. Include a selection of these in the display.

◆ Children can plan their own story drawing a main character, a setting and a beginning, middle and end. Provide a worksheet for this with boxes in which the children can sketch out the above.

◆ Get the children to use their story plans to write a story or tell a story into a tape recorder. These could be transcribed by an adult, word-processed and illustrated by the children themselves and made into a class collection.

◆ Ask the children to make a list of instructions about how to grow or make a good friendship. Look first at instructions for making a cake, or growing a plant from a seed or bulb and then encourage them to write in the same style about developing a friendship.

◆ Ask the children to write about their best friend but without naming them, and to make their descriptions into riddles for the other children to guess who they are about. Look at riddles first with the children to help them to do this.

◆ Write a class poem about friends.

◆ In pairs, ask the children to discuss their own ending to the story and retell it to the rest of the class. Reiterate the real ending of the story with the children.

Keeping safe

This theme is a key component of the PSHE and citizenship syllabus, but there are aspects of keeping safe that are sensitive and difficult to deliver at Key Stage 1, in particular the focus on child protection issues. The issue of Stranger Danger and unwanted physical contact in the home environment are best tackled in whole-class, planned, supported presentation and discussion. The Local Authority Adviser on child protection, along with the police, may be helpful contacts to assist in this topic. Therefore, it has not been addressed in this chapter except obliquely in relation to getting help. Instead, the following texts deal with fear and the management of that defence emotion, the current problem of hoax calls to the fire brigade and raising awareness of dangers inside and out of the house. The use of Humpty Dumpty is concentrated on the risks that come from dangerous play. It encourages the children to make some sort of basic risk assessment before playing dangerously.

The whole emphasis of any work undertaken in this area is that of a positive approach. Areas of potential dangers are highlighted but only alongside strategies for keeping safe. The preventative thrust is significant at this age because empowerment is needed to avoid frightening children unnecessarily. At the same time a young child must be confident of getting help from an adult rather than attempting always to solve their own safety problems.

Matilda Who Told Such Dreadful Lies...

Genre
rhyming poem with a moral tale by a significant author

Matilda told such Dreadful Lies,
It made one Gasp and Stretch one's Eyes;
…
For once, towards the Close of Day,
Matilda, growing tired of play,
And finding she was left alone…
Went tiptoe to the Telephone
And summoned the Immediate Aid
Of London's Noble Fire Brigade.
Within an hour the Gallant Band
Were pouring in on every hand,
From Putney, Hackney Downs and Bow,
With Courage high and Hearts a-glow
They galloped, roaring through the Town…
"Matilda's House is Burning Down!"

by Hilaire Belloc

Matilda Who Told Such Dreadful Lies...

Make a display called *People who help us — the fire brigade*. Add rules in the event of a fire.

PSHE and citizenship learning objectives

◆ To recognise what is right and wrong (1a).

◆ To recognise choices can be made (2c).

◆ To understand how rules help (2d).

◆ To know some of the rules for, and ways of, keeping safe, including fire safety, and about people who can help us to stay safe (3g).

◆ To recognise how behaviour affects other people (4a).

◆ To know how to ask for help in the event of a fire (5h).

Background notes

This poem dates from the late Victorian period and was the type of gruesome moral tale told to scare children into being good. 'Matilda' is a poem that warns of the dangers of lying. Belloc uses a 'cry wolf' situation which strangely has resonance with today's society. In the full poem Matilda gets burned to death when the house catches fire. Having previously lied about the house being on fire, she is universally ignored when the real fire breaks out. Obviously for infant children this scenario may be too violent. Thus, because of the dramatic and grotesque outcome in this poem, only the first few verses have been given in this extract, stopping the text at a point where children can speculate about the problems Matilda is causing by her dishonesty. The poem, however, introduces the children to Hilaire Belloc and to a very fine example of rhyming couplets.

Vocabulary

Fire brigade, firefighter, lies, emergency service, ambulance, police.

Discussing the text

◆ Confirm with the children that they understand what is happening in this poem using questioning, for example *What has Matilda done? Why did she call the fire brigade?* Refer back to the text for content clues. Establish that Matilda often lied. She phoned the fire brigade though there was no fire.

◆ Ask the children why they think Matilda did this. Refer back to the text again but also accept their creative ideas (she was naughty, she was bored, she wanted to cause trouble). Point out that she was left alone and had the chance to be naughty.

◆ Explore with the children the moral root of the story. What did Maltilda do wrong? (Lie and waste the time of an emergency service — there could be a real child in a burning house who was in danger because the fire engine was at Matilda's house.)

◆ Ask the children to talk to the person next to them and come up with some ideas about what might happen next. What would the chief firefighter say to Matilda? Would her aunt (explain that is who she lived with) punish her? Get the children to share their ideas and write down the possible plot developments on a flip chart.

◆ Consider with the children how the people involved in the story might have felt. How did Matilda feel after the fire brigade came? (Sorry? Pleased with herself? Unrepentant?) Record suggestions on a flip chart. Ask a confident child to pretend he or she is Matilda and say how she feels. How do the children think Matilda's aunt would feel? Again see if a child can act out or articulate those feelings in front of the class and record key feeling words on the flip chart. Finally, ask children to think about what the firefighters felt. Record and act out suggestions if possible.

◆ Ask the children what would happen if, after all this, Matilda really was caught in a fire at home and tried to summon help from the fire brigade, or from people in the street? (They may not believe her and then refuse to come.) Make the moral point that if we lie a lot we may find it hard to get people to believe us when we are telling the truth.

PSHE and citizenship activities

◆ Get children to work with a partner to write or draw what they think the next part of the story might be. (Look for understanding of the moral implications of the story.)

◆ Ask children to work out a maxim about the importance of telling the truth which they can design as a poster for display. For example *Always tell the truth and you will be believed*; *Lying is wrong*; *The truth is best*.

◆ Read and discuss with the class the folk story of 'The Boy Who Cried Wolf' to reaffirm the principle of being honest and the dangers of habitual lying. Focus on the positive – if you tell the truth people will trust and believe you. Stress that even when we are in trouble or have done something wrong it is better to tell the truth. Also point out that we all like to be with people who are truthful and who do not lie to us.

◆ Ask a firefighter to come in and talk to the children about his or her job, fire safety in the house and school, and nuisance calls. Make a major point about the difference between deliberately lying to the fire brigade and calling them because you think there is a genuine fire. Do follow-up work on basic rules and what the children should do if they feel that there is a fire in the house. Get them to write out these rules using the word processor. Enlarge these for displaying.

◆ Ask the children to work out, with their family, a safe route out of the house and practise it.

◆ Think about emergency situations with the children. Who do they think would be best to get help from? List a number of situations on the flip chart and write the right emergency service category next to each.

Further literacy ideas

◆ Ask the children to write a set of instructions for dialing 999 and summoning the fire brigade, ambulance or police.

◆ Look at *ow* sounds in the text with the children and get them to sort these into different phoneme groups (for example, *ough*, *ow*, *ou*). How many different graphemes make the phoneme *ow*? (*Cow*, *out*, *bough*.) Compile a list and store them in a class wordbank.

◆ Ask the children to write a humorous poem full of exaggerated lies about themselves, for example *I am as tall as a house*.

◆ Write a class letter to thank the firefighter for coming in to talk to the children.

◆ Get the children to compile a newspaper report about Matilda's naughtiness and her punishment.

◆ Look at the poem again and focus on how the poet has used capital letters. Discuss with the children the usual convention for capitals in poetry. Why has the poet used so many capitals do they think? (To add emphasis to certain words.)

Safety signs

Genre
labels and
signs with
captions

Steep hill upwards

Swing bridge ahead

River bank

Traffic calming ahead

Loose chippings

Slippery road

School crossing

Do not iron

Machine wash in
warm water at a
normal setting

Fire exit

Fire extinguisher

Fire alarm call point

Toxic

High voltage electricity

Poisonous

TEACHERS' NOTES

Safety signs

Display a large set of labels with matching explanations for children to match to the right sign.

PSHE and citizenship learning objectives

◆ To realise that people and other living things have needs, and that they have responsibilities to meet them (2e).

◆ To contribute to the life of the class and the school (2h).

◆ To be able to make simple choices that improve health or well-being (3a).

◆ To know that all household products can be harmful if not used properly (3f).

◆ To know the rules for, and ways of, keeping safe, including basic road safety, and about people who can help us to stay safe (3g).

◆ To recognise how behaviour affects other people (4a).

◆ To recognise that family and friends should care for each other (4d).

◆ To know how to ask for help (5h).

Background notes

Warning and safety signs are all around us. Young children can often 'read' them and understand the dangers or hazards that they caution.

Vocabulary

Sign, label, warning, safety.

Discussing the text

◆ Identify what type of writing is in the text with the children (labels, signs, symbols and instructions). Ask the children what they have in common. What is their common purpose? (To warn people of dangers and therefore prevent accidents.)

◆ Discuss safety signs and labels the children might have seen or can remember, such as *fire exit* or *way out*. Record these on a flip chart.

◆ Ask the children what is important when writing warning labels and signs (short clear words or pictures that help people understand quickly and easily, even if they cannot read). Use of colour or shape might be raised also – *bright* or *red* or *triangle* or *circle*. If these issues are raised, ask the children why they think red is used quite so often. (To symbolise danger, or the association with the red 'stop' light.)

◆ Discuss with the children why we need warning labels and signs. How do they help to keep us safe? (They make sure that people know that they must be careful, that something or some situation could be unsafe.)

◆ Make a list of dangers in the classroom and playground with the children (such as sharp corners, door hinges, steps, tarmac). Ask for one or two suggestions for possible warning signs or labels for these.

◆ Discuss possible dangers the children might find at home and ways for keeping safe, for example climbing into a bath of water that is too hot – get an adult to check the temperature of the water before getting into the bath.

PSHE and citizenship activities

◆ Record on the flip chart, safety signs and labels in a column on the left-hand side. Then invite individual children to write or draw on the right-hand side simple words that explain the sign, for example *Do not touch the wire it will hurt you.*

◆ In pairs, ask the children to design warning signs with bright colours and simple, direct text or symbols for the classroom and the playground. Use these around the classroom and in the corridor leading to the playground to alert other children of risks.

◆ Ask the children to look at home and when outdoors or travelling, for signs and warnings. Pictures of the signs they have seen and explanations about the dangers can then be painted in the classroom and displayed. Children could go out in a group, with supervision, to take photos of warning signs to be used in a display.

◆ Bring into the classroom a community police officer or schools liaison police officer to talk about keeping safe and getting help if the children are in difficulty or are frightened.

◆ Ask the children to talk about safety at home, especially in the kitchen. What should they be careful about? (Electricity, poisons and medicines, hot things in the kitchen, hot water in the bathroom, fires and matches.) Groups of children could choose a room in the house, and the garden, to point out potential dangers and the right things to do to keep themselves and their family safe.

Further literacy ideas

◆ Make a class poster showing safe ways of doing things at school or in the home.

◆ Ask the children to write a story in which they stop another child from doing something unsafe.

◆ Ask the children to suggest, and make a collection of, stories about heroes and heroines rescuing people from dangerous situations such as Grace Darling. These could be fiction or non-fiction, historical or contemporary.

◆ Show the children road safety signs in a foreign country from a road atlas and get them to match them to British road safety signs.

◆ Using the word *dangerous*, how many new words can the children make?

◆ Ask the children to compile pairs of antonyms, for example *dangerous/safe, hot/cold, sharp/blunt.*

Humpty Dumpty

PHOTOCOPIABLE

Genre
nursery
rhyme

Humpty Dumpty sat on a wall.
Humpty Dumpty had a great fall.
All the King's horses and all the King's men
couldn't put Humpty together again.

Humpty Dumpty looked at the wall
He stopped and thought. It was too tall.
He walked away to find a place
That he could enjoy and was also safe.

Humpty Dumpty

Display a big three-window display. Humpty on the wall on the left, with the words of the rhyme; then a picture of Humpty injured and bandaged on the ground; finally a 'safe' alternative picture of Humpty standing by the wall with a speech bubble saying *This wall is too high. I might fall and hurt myself if I climb on it. I will find a friend to play with instead.*

PSHE and citizenship learning objectives

◆ To recognise choices can be made, and recognise the difference between right and wrong (2c).
◆ To recognise how simple choices can improve health and well-being (3a).
◆ To know some of the rules for, and ways of, keeping safe (3g).
◆ To recognise that family and friends should care for each another (4d).
◆ To take and share responsibility for behaviour (5a).
◆ To make real choices about keeping safe (5d).

Background notes

This popular and very familiar nursery rhyme is useful to illustrate the problems of dangerous play. An alternative rhyme has also been included to illustrate the strategy of risk assessment and the selection of a safer playground.

Vocabulary

Too high, hurt, injured, dangerous, safe, climb.

Discussing the text

◆ Read the first, more traditional nursery rhyme. Ask the children why Humpty fell off the wall. *Was he being silly? Was he showing off to his friends?* Compile a range of possible reasons on a flip chart (he wanted to see if he could climb up high, he wanted to show off, he wanted to see something a long way away, he wanted to rest, he wanted to prove how brave he was).

◆ Discuss the reasons with the children why Humpty was so badly hurt from the fall (because the wall was too high – it was dangerous for Humpty to climb up onto the wall in the first place).

◆ Ask the children if they have had an accident falling from a high place. Stress the danger of being up high.

◆ Identify what Humpty should have done when he saw the wall. Using a picture of Humpty standing looking at the wall with an attached thought bubble, ask the children for some ideas about what he is thinking. Write these in the thought bubble. Read the second, alternative verse at this point with the children. Identify Humpty's desire to climb, his awareness that it might be too high and he could get hurt, then his decision to do something else instead.

◆ Discuss safe places where the children can play and climb, for example the park where there is a soft woodchip floor, or in the garden with someone watching over them.

PSHE and citizenship activities

◆ Children can create a safe picture storyboard with three pictures. The first shows Humpty looking at the wall with a thought bubble. The second shows Humpty walking away with a thought bubble. The final picture is of Humpty playing on the climbing frame in a play park with a thought bubble. Add these storyboards to the display.

◆ In pairs, the children can compose an alternative verse to the rhyme with a safe and happy ending, like the second rhyme in the text. This can be produced on the word processor for part of the display.

◆ In groups, get the children to role-play being a good friend and stopping their playmate from climbing onto something that could be dangerous.

◆ Visit the play park or the Foundation Stage play area with the class and look at the way the play area is made safer. Look at the flooring, the strong and secure apparatus, the fence and the range of different climbing frames to suit different ages. Take a photo and discuss it further back in the classroom.

◆ Children, in pairs or groups, can design their own climbing frame for the playground or park pointing out the safety features. Send their designs to the local council with a class-produced letter composed using an OHT, then typed on a word processor.

◆ Get the children to create a large-scale collage or painting for the display of Humpty with both the traditional ending and a safer ending.

Further literacy ideas

◆ Ask the children to look at the *um*, *ump* or *mpty* words in the text. Record them on the flip chart and then list similar words that the children can think of. Record them all in a class wordbank.

◆ Encourage the children to learn off by heart the Humpty Dumpty rhyme with actions. Learn other nursery rhymes together and create a performance of nursery rhymes with actions for the rest of the school.

◆ Ask the children to write the story of Humpty from his parents' point of view.

◆ Ask the children to write a poem with an alternate line rhyming scheme, using scaffolded text where the lines are given except the second matching rhyme line.

◆ Write a collective letter of complaint to the local council about the unsafe equipment or absence of safe play equipment in the park.

Keeping safe in the home

Medicines

Sometimes we need to take special medicines like tablets or syrups. We have to take these when we are sick. They make us better. Tablets can look like sweets but they are not sweets. We must not eat them unless Mum, or Dad, or our carer says we should. Syrups can taste nice but we must not drink them unless Mum, or Dad, or our carer says that we can. If we find any tablets or syrups we must give them to an adult.

DANGEROUS LIQUIDS

In the kitchen

There are all sorts of bottles of liquids in the kitchen. Many are kept under the sink.

They are not drinks.

They are used to clean things in the house.

They are poisonous.

They may burn us or make us very, very sick if we drink from them.

If we see these signs we should leave the bottles alone.

In the bathroom

The toilet is cleaned with a thick liquid called toilet cleaner or bleach.

It is unsafe to touch this liquid. It can burn our skin or get in our eyes. We must not drink it. It will make us very sick.

If some spills then we need to get an adult to clear it up.

Bottles that are found in the bathroom should not be drunk.

In the garden shed

Sometimes the shed has liquids and powders that are put on the grass, or the earth, or the stones to get rid of pests or weeds. These can be very poisonous.

We should not touch anything in the shed without an adult there.

Keeping safe in the home

Display a list of the instructions in the text with illustrations provided by the children. Surround with examples of their own instructions on how to keep safe.

PSHE and citizenship learning objectives

◆ To recognise what is right and wrong (1a).

◆ To recognise choices can be made (2c).

◆ To make simple choices that improve health and well-being (3a).

◆ To know that all household products can be harmful if not used properly (3f).

◆ To know the rules for, and ways of, keeping safe and about people who can help us stay safe (3g).

◆ To take and share responsibility (5a).

◆ To take part in discussions (5c).

◆ To be able to ask for help (5h).

Vocabulary

Unsafe, dangerous, medicines, poisonous.

Discussing the text

◆ Ask the children what sort of writing this is an example of (instruction and explanation). Why is that? (It contains direct orders to the reader and reasons why those orders need to be followed.)

◆ Look at the first section in detail. What sentences do the children think are explaining things? What sentences are instructing? (Those that state *do* or *do not*.) Get them to highlight with different-coloured pens which sentences are doing what.

◆ Ask the children to read the text with you. Test comprehension by asking the children about what is dangerous and where the dangerous things are. Check with them why must we not take medicines without permission.

◆ When looking at the bathroom and garden sections, ask confident children to role-play the scenarios.

◆ With a soft toy, puppet or teddy demonstrate telling Teddy off or warning Teddy to stop doing something unsafe in each of the locations. Ask the children why Teddy is doing something dangerous. (Because he's curious, or thinks that it is something nice, such as sweets.)

◆ Discuss with the children if there is another way these instructions could be written, for example as a list with numbered points, or with picture illustrations. Get them to translate one of the sections into a bullet pointed list.

PSHE and citizenship activities

◆ To reinforce the children's understanding of the text ask them to work in pairs to rewrite one of the sections of text as a bulleted list. They can draw pictures to illustrate the scenes.

◆ Children could do large-scale paintings of the warning signs on bottles for corrosive, toxic, harmful liquids. Children can use the word processor to make up their own simple explanations of these signs.

◆ Ask the children to get a parent to show them where the dangerous liquids are kept in their home. Ask them to locate the danger sign on the bottles.

◆ Ask the children to write a story in the first person about a younger brother or sister playing under the sink and intending to drink from some of the bottles there. What would they do and say to stop them?

◆ Discuss with the children strategies to put into action if they accidentally swallowed something they shouldn't and it makes them feel very sick or it burns them (get help from an adult very quickly).

◆ Tell the children a story of a child who does swallow something and has to go to the hospital and is very sick, to illustrate the dangers in an imaginative way.

◆ Present a display of empty washed-out bottles bearing the danger signs. Ask the children to attach the right product type and location in the home to the right bottle.

Further literacy ideas

◆ Look at other explanatory texts with the class. Identify the important features (short instructions, clearly understood words).

◆ Ask the children to illustrate each of the sections in the text in a pictorial cartoon format for children who can't read.

◆ The children can design their own labels warning people not to touch or drink certain products.

◆ Design a class leaflet focusing on instruction words: *don't…*, *never…*, *always…*, and so on.

◆ Children can write their own explanations about dangerous liquids in the home, choosing whichever room in the house they want.

◆ Look at *oi* phonemes in words with the children, using *poisons* as an example. Ask them to find other words using this digraph and make a class wordbank.

◆ Make a class wordsearch using words like *poison, liquid, danger, bleach, corrosive,* that may be found on labels.

Owl Babies

Genre
picture book, narrative fiction

Introduction to the text

This is a story about three baby owls: Sarah, the oldest, Percy and Bill, the youngest. They wake up in the middle of the night and find their mother has gone from their home in the tree. They are very frightened.

It was dark in the wood and they had to be brave, for things *moved* all around them.
"She'll bring us mice and things that are nice," said Sarah.
"I suppose so!" said Percy.
"I want my mummy!" said Bill.
They sat and they thought (all owls think a lot) –
"I think we should *all* sit on *my* branch," said Sarah.
And they did,
all three together.
"Suppose she got lost," said Sarah.
"Or a fox got her!" said Percy.
"I want my mummy!" said Bill.
And the baby owls closed
Their owl eyes and wished their
Owl Mother would come.

Owl Babies

Display pictures, photographs and replicas of owls and their habitat.

PSHE and citizenship learning objectives

◆ To recognise belonging to various groups and communities, such as family and school. (2f).

◆ To understand rules for, and ways of, keeping safe, including basic road safety, and about people who can help us to stay safe (3g).

◆ To recognise that family and friends should care for each another (4d).

Background notes

This is a lovely story that explores issues of fear, particularly fear of the dark. This extract shows how the eldest child can help the younger ones cope with their fears. In this way the family helps itself to cope.

Vocabulary

Frightened, scared, worried, owl, dark, safe.

Discussing the text

◆ Ask the children what they know about owls, such as what they are, where they live and what they like to eat. Are they night creatures (nocturnal), or do they fly about in the day? Discuss what nocturnal means. Support a discussion with pictures of owls in the wild and a collection of twigs and leaves. Ask the children to imagine what an owl's nest feels like and what it would be like to live in an owl's nest. What is their bedroom like? How can they make their bedroom cosy?

◆ Ask the children who the main characters in the story are. *What is the relationship between them? Who is in the children's family? Why are families special?*

◆ Ask the children why they think the mother owl has gone. Look at the reasons the baby owls give for their mother's departure. Are they sensible or likely reasons?

◆ Discuss the feelings of each of the owl characters, Percy, Sarah and Bill with the children. Record them on a flip chart. What similarities and differences can the children see between them? Ask which of the baby owls they think is the bravest and the most confident, and which the most frightened. Ask them to speculate about why Sarah is so confident and why Bill is the most scared.

◆ Ask the children to think about a time when they have felt like this (sad and frightened, worried or lonely). How did they make themselves feel better, or what made them feel better?

◆ Ask the children if they think the owls were frightened because it was dark. *Why do the owls not need to be frightened of the dark?* Are the children frightened of the dark? Reassure them that they do not need to be.

◆ Ask the children to predict what will happen at the end of the story.

PSHE and citizenship activities

◆ Make a list on the flip chart identifying the dangers facing the baby owls and ask the children to suggest how the owls could keep safe. Divide the children into four groups, and working in pairs within the group, ask them to list ways of keeping safe in one of the following situations: in the home, out shopping, out playing and on holiday. Then get them to share their ideas with the whole class. Follow this by making safety posters of the ideas.

◆ Ask the children to tell each other (in pairs) what to do if they get lost or separated from their parents or carers. Work through the basic principles of finding a police officer, a shopkeeper, or woman with children, and getting help. Help the children to learn their full name and address and, if possible, their telephone number. The children could practise this and show the rest of the class that they know it.

◆ The children could act out the scenarios of getting lost and getting help.

◆ Get the children to draw a picture of Bill and put inside him the words that describe how he felt. They could do the same for the mother owl. Ask them to write on the bottom of the picture what would make Bill feel better.

◆ Ask the children to tell a friend about a time when they felt frightened. Ask the friend to tell them what they would do to help. Suggest ways in which the children can help themselves be less afraid.

◆ Teach the class some cheering, helpful songs, such as 'Whistle A Happy Tune' from *The King and I*, or 'My favourite things' from *The Sound of Music*.

◆ Get the children to make soft owls from pompoms or cotton wool in three different sizes, then to retell the story using the figures with a child playing the mother owl.

◆ Get the children to paint or draw a picture of the special people in their lives, or their family. Ask them to write down why these people are special and how they help one another.

◆ The children can paint a picture of the story, then write the end of the story as a short narrative, perhaps using the word processor.

◆ Find out from the RSPB about endangered species of owls in Britain and what can be done to help them.

Further literacy ideas

◆ Ask the children to write a set of *Keep safe* rules (procedural text), incorporating their work on keeping safe at home, and when out playing, from earlier in this chapter.

◆ Ask the children to identify feeling words from a discussion of the text. Put these onto separate cards and sort the cards into two categories, adjectives and verbs. The children can add their own words.

◆ Use the first chapter of *The Owl Who Was Afraid of the Dark* by Jill Tomlinson to compare the feelings of the owl with the baby owls in this text. This links to children being afraid themselves and, in Tomlinson's work, further chapters look at how the problem is resolved.

◆ Read the end of the story again and compare it with the children's own predictions. Which do they like the best?

◆ Ask the children to write a speech by the mother owl to make the owls feel better.

◆ Gather together a collection of information books about owls. The children could make their own *All About Owls* class reference book, using reference books, CD-ROMs and the Internet.

◆ The children could visit a wildlife sanctuary, or write to the RSPB, to find out about what owls need to live and the different types of native owls there are.

◆ Encourage the children to create their own web page about owls.

Keeping healthy

As young children grow up and become more responsible for their own actions, we need to equip them with the knowledge to make safe, sensible, informed choices about how to look after themselves and stay healthy. In this chapter, children are introduced to the concepts of what we need to do to be healthy, what our bodies need and how we can look after our bodies through attention to hygiene, exercise and what we eat.

The programme of study for PSHE and citizenship for this area is broad. It aims to develop in the children a range of knowledge, from being able to name the main parts of the body to making healthy choices about food, and participating in and enjoying exercise. There are many close links with the National Curriculum for science and physical education. The area of study also provides many opportunities to develop a whole-school approach and looking at keeping healthy could be extended into the wider community, involving parents, grandparents, and so on. Some sensitive issues will also be raised in the discussion and activities for some of the texts, such as headlice, weight and identifying poor eating habits. You will need to be aware of any children or families for whom these may be difficult, for example those who regularly have headlice, those who are less clean, or those who have a particularly over- or underweight parent or carer. And although we are encouraging a healthy diet we are not encouraging dieting. Children need to be taught that a healthy diet here is balancing what we eat, not restricting what we eat.

Throughout, children are encouraged to look at their lifestyles and to alter their choices where necessary to ensure they develop a healthier way of life. If we can encourage informed sensible choices at an early age, children will grow up to be healthier young adults.

Willy the Wimp

Genre
narrative
fiction by a
well-known
author

Introduction

Willy is a chimp who is fed up with being smaller than the rest of his friends and being picked on because of his size. One day Willy spots an advert for an exercise programme to make him bigger and stronger. He decides that he is ready to try anything and so he sends for the book. Eventually it arrives through the post and Willy discovers what he has to do to become big and strong like the other chimps.

First some exercises.
Then some jogging.
Willy had to go on a special diet.
He went to aerobics classes where everybody danced to disco music.
Willy felt a bit silly.

by Anthony Browne

Willy the Wimp

Display books about healthy eating and exercise.

PSHE and citizenship learning objectives

◆ To know how to set simple goals (1e).

◆ To be able to take part in a simple debate about topical issues (2b).

◆ To understand how to make simple choices that improve health and well-being (3a).

◆ To know about the process of growing from young to old and how people's needs change (3d).

◆ To recognise the names of the main parts of the body (3e).

◆ To feel positive about ourselves (5b).

◆ To make real choices, for example between healthy options in school meals (5d).

Vocabulary

Keeping fit, being healthy, exercise.

Discussing the text

◆ Ask the children what they think the book that came for Willy was about. Why do they think Willy wanted a book like this? What was it going to help him to do?

◆ Discuss with the children how they think Willy felt before and after using the book. Ask them how they feel after playing out, PE, playing football, swimming, and so on.

◆ Do the children know the name for the things Willy has been doing? (Exercise.) Why do people do these sorts of things?

◆ What do the children think happened to Willy in the end? Explain that in the book he becomes big and strong in just a few months. Do they think this could really happen? Discuss with them how we do not need to be big to be strong and healthy, small people can be strong too. Are there any children in the class or school who are small and strong? (For example, on the school football team or in the gymnastics club.)

◆ Discuss with the children how we become fit and healthy. Talk about exercise, playing out and eating well.

PSHE and citizenship activities

◆ Make a tally chart of the physical activities the children do regularly. Ask them to find out at home who does regular exercise and what it is. Use this information to make graphs showing how people keep fit and display these.

◆ Get the children to write about what physical activities they like to do, for example swimming,

◆ Use non-fiction texts with the children to find out why we need to exercise. Ask the children to write an explanation in their own words.

◆ The children can design a mini-exercise circuit using familiar apparatus from their PE lessons, such as hoops, beanbags, skipping ropes, and so on. Get them to draw their designs onto paper so others can have a go at the exercise.

◆ Investigate how many hops, jumps, skips and catches the children can do and ask them to record their findings. They can practise and test themselves again later in the term to see if they have managed any improvements.

◆ Discuss with the children the parts of the body we use when exercising. Encourage them to learn the names of these parts and to draw labelled diagrams showing which parts are used in which exercises. These could be made into a class poster.

◆ Discuss what might have been included in Willy's special diet and teach the children how important it is that we get a balanced, healthy diet. Discuss the main food groups and how we need some of each of these every day. Get the children to make a collage or drawing of their favourite meal on a paper plate. Reinforce the fact that sweets and chocolate, and chips and crisps are all fine but we should not eat too much of each every day.

◆ Encourage the children to discuss what would be a healthy choice each day for their school dinner or packed lunch. Make class posters advertising these healthy options. Get the children to keep a diary for a week of what they have eaten as snacks and at lunchtime. They can make graphs to show this information.

◆ If you have a school tuck shop, write a class letter to whoever runs it suggesting ways of providing a healthy selection.

◆ In cookery sessions, make some healthy option biscuits, for example by using a recipe with dried fruit in it. Encourage the children to take the recipe home.

◆ Set up a class café and help the children to design healthy menus. Provide all the necessary resources for a role-play area, such as tables, menus, an order pad, and so on. Involve the children in making pretend food with dough, then leaving it to harden and painting it.

Further literacy ideas

◆ Consider with the children the verbs linked to exercising in the text, starting with the examples jogging and dancing and then discuss others, for example playing, jumping and running. Children can add to this list. Make lists of these verbs using the suffixes -ing and -ed and finding the root word, for example jogging, jogged, jog; running, ran, run. This can be done as a whole-class activity or an independent activity.

◆ Ask the children to predict what will happen to Willy if he continues to follow this programme. Will it make a big difference to his life? (He will be able to stick up for himself.) Lead the children towards considering what sorts of things they can do if they are fit that they might not be able to do if they aren't. They can write a comparative list of things they can or can't do.

◆ The children can write their own diary of activities they do each week after school, for example playing out, swimming, football, tennis, watching TV. Get them to write about which parts of the body the different activities they do exercise.

You are what you eat!

Genre
*non-fiction
explanation
text*

We all need to eat so that our bodies work and to help us to grow.
It is important that we eat sensible food and we need to eat all sorts of
different types of food.

Each type of food helps our bodies in different ways.

Some foods help our bones and bodies to grow bigger and stronger.

Some foods give us energy each day to help us to work and play, and to
help our bodies to work properly.

We also need foods to help us store energy for when we get tired or ill.

As well as eating food we need to drink lots. Water, milk and fruit juices
are good for us.

The food we eat each day is called our diet and we need to eat all types of
food to have a healthy diet.

We need to be careful not to eat too much of some kinds of foods.
Too many sweets, fatty foods and fizzy drinks will rot our teeth, make our
skin spotty and make us get bigger too quickly.

by Jackie Barbera

You are what you eat!

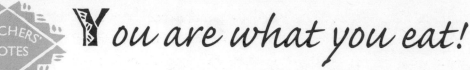

Make a display of different food groups using empty packets, fruit and vegetable replicas, tins, and so on.

PSHE and citizenship learning objectives

◆ To recognise likes and dislikes (1a).
◆ To think about ourselves, learn from experiences and recognise what we are good at (1d).
◆ To know how to set simple goals (1e).
◆ To be able to take part in a simple debate about topical issues (2b).
◆ To recognise choices can be made (2c).
◆ To realise that people and other living things have needs (2e).
◆ To know how to make simple choices that improve health and well-being (3a).
◆ To be able to make real choices (5d).
◆ To be able to consider social and moral dilemmas in everyday life (5g).

Vocabulary

Food, healthy, good, bad, variety (for older children the food groups of proteins, dairy products and carbohydrates, fruit and vegetables, fatty foods, fibre).

Discussing the text

◆ Read the text with the children and focus on the food groups and why we need to eat them. Go through each of the different types of food, discussing what they are and looking at examples (try to give older children the proper names for the food groups, *proteins*, *dairy products* or *carbohydrates*; with younger children stick to the explanation in the text). If you have made a collection of foods for a display, use these to illustrate the discussion.
◆ Discuss why water is good for us. (It helps our food digest and flushes out impurities.) Ask the children if any of them drink water on its own. This can be from a tap or a bottle. Do they enjoy it?
◆ Explain to the children that we need a variety of all the foods to keep healthy. Discuss with them what *healthy* means. (Having energy, having good skin and hair and so on.)
◆ Talk with the children about the type of foods that can be bad for us (sugary and fatty foods). Emphasise that we all need to eat some foods with sugar and fat in them, but it is important not to eat too much of these foods or to eat them too often.

PSHE and citizenship learning activities

◆ In pairs, ask the children to share what their last meal before the lesson was (it could be breakfast or lunch depending on the time of day, or snacks if the lesson is after playtime). Choose a few children to tell the class about what they have eaten. Record the information on a flip chart and as a class try to sort the foods into groups. Make no judgement about what the children have eaten, just explore the range and types of food. Then get the children to work in groups of four and repeat the activity for themselves. Start by getting individuals to make a list of what they ate or to draw pictures to remind themselves. Then, in their groups, they can discuss what they each had and try to put the food into the correct groups and make a chart to display the information. Compare the charts of each group once they have finished. Do they look the same or are there differences? Are the children generally healthy eaters or not? Are there some things most children eat or drink too much of, for example crisps and coke? Are there things they aren't eating enough of, for example fruit or vegetables?

◆ Ask the children to keep a log of what they eat for a few days. Make small food diaries for them to fill in after each meal or snack, and write a note to parents explaining what you are doing and asking for their support at dinner- and suppertime. Remember that some children with dietary needs, or who are diabetic, may need regular snacks and will need to do this activity more often – be sensitive to this. However, it may be a good opportunity to discuss with the children how some people have special food needs and why a particular child in the class is allowed to eat at times when others are not, such as during afternoon play.

◆ Using the food diaries, the children can make individual charts of which types of food they eat, and how often and how much of the food groups they are eating. They can then try to decide if they have a healthy diet. Discuss with them ways of getting more of the foods they don't eat enough of, for example fruit and vegetables. You can also advise them on how to reduce their eating of too many bad foods, such as crisps or sweets. Get them to set simple individual goals for improving their diet (they may need to share these goals at home to be able to do it, such as asking for an apple for a snack two days a week instead of crisps).

◆ In groups, ask the children to design a healthy menu of one day's meals for a child of their age. Display these or use them in a play café.

◆ Investigate with the children what their favourite drinks are and what they drink the most of. Look at which drinks are better for us and explain why it is important that we drink water and milk to help our organs, bones and teeth. With older children, you could discuss dehydration and its effects. Some children may not like milk so discuss alternative ways of getting calcium (yoghurt, fromage frais, cheese and cereals). Use the information collected to make bar charts to show favourite drinks. Ask the children to make posters reminding everyone to drink plenty of water and display these near the water fountains or taps used for drinking water. Look at how the school caters for this. Could it be improved, especially in the summer when we need to drink more?

Further literacy ideas

◆ In pairs, get the children to design a leaflet explaining how to eat a healthy diet. These can then be given out to children in other classes by photocopying them, or printing more copies if they are word-processed (the children could also take a copy home to inform parents). Display the originals.

◆ Make a collection of menus from a variety of restaurants and cafés. Look with the children at how a menu is set out. Discuss what a starter, main course and sweet are, and what extras there may be, such as side orders. The children can make their own menus based on their favourite foods and use these in a role-play café or restaurant area.

◆ Talk with the children about appropriate behaviour in a café or restaurant. Explain how to ask for food, how orders are taken, and so on. The children can role-play being both the customer and the waiter or waitress, using good manners in each role. Talk about 'proper' ways of talking linked to standard English and compare these with slang for common phrases that may be used in this situation and others. Make a list of these to display, such as *ta/thank you, gi'us/could I please have*.

◆ Look with the children at nouns and adjectives linked to food. Ask them to write about their favourite food, making their descriptions enticing and mouth-watering, for example a piece of sticky, gooey chocolate cake or a crisp, crunchy, green apple. They can then write descriptions of a food without actually saying what it is. Display these and see whether other children can guess what food is being described. Alternatively, they could be made into little books with a lift-the-flap section which has the answer behind it.

Genre
instructional
text

Pasta house

Use celery sticks for trees.

Make your house on a foil-covered tray.

You will need:

200g (8oz) of pasta twists in three colours

celery

strips of cucumber for window frames

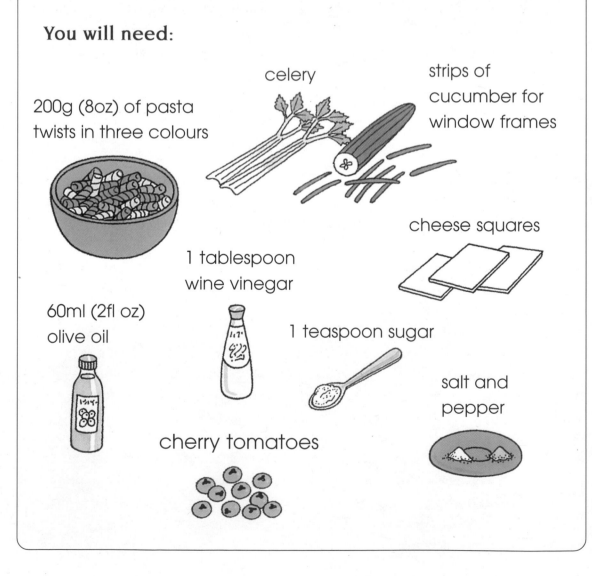

cheese squares

1 tablespoon wine vinegar

60ml (2fl oz) olive oil

1 teaspoon sugar

salt and pepper

cherry tomatoes

1.

Boil the pasta shapes in salted water for about 8 minutes. Ask someone to do this for you.

2.

Mix the sugar, salt, pepper and vinegar in a jug. Slowly add the olive oil, beating with a fork.

3.

Ask an adult to drain the pasta and put it in a bowl. Pour on the dressing and let the pasta cool.

4.

Make your house. Start with the frame and then fill in. Use cheese for the door and windows.

by J Bastyra and C Bradley
illustrated by Michael Evans

Pasta house

Collect together all the ingredients and utensils required in the recipe. Display these and refer to them whilst discussing the text.

PSHE and citizenship learning objectives

◆ To recognise likes and dislikes (1a).

◆ To share opinions on things that matter to us (1b).

◆ To be able to set simple goals (1e).

◆ To take part in a simple debate about topical issues (2b).

◆ To recognise choices can be made (2c).

◆ To agree and follow rules for the group and classroom, and understand how rules help (2d).

◆ To maintain personal hygiene (3b).

◆ To learn to take and share responsibility (5a).

◆ To be able to ask for help (5h).

Background notes

Encourage children to take an interest in what they eat and how it is made. This text is a recipe for a healthy meal which is made to look more interesting, giving children encouragement to help make it and eat it. The focus is also on how to maintain hygiene during food preparation.

Vocabulary

Recipe, ingredients, instructions, being safe, pasta, celery, olive oil, wine vinegar, pan, boil, jug, drain.

Discussing the text

◆ Look at the title of the text and the picture of the pasta house with the children. What do they think the rest of the text will be about? What clues are there in the general layout? What do we call this type of text (a recipe)?

◆ Ask the children how many of them have used a recipe before. Where? With whom? What did they make?

◆ Look at the main picture only and ask the children what they think the recipe will be giving instructions to do. (Make sure they know what the term *instructions* means.) Ask a few children to look closely at the picture and focus their attention on what they think has been used to make the different parts of the house and garden.

◆ Focus on the *You will need* section of the text. Introduce the term *ingredients* to the children. Can they tell you what they will need to make the pasta house? If you have already made a collection of ingredients and utensils use these to support the discussion. Go through each ingredient and discuss what it is.

◆ Look at the instructions for making the pasta house. Ask the children how many steps to the recipe there are. Read each one in turn discussing what they would have to do if they were following this recipe. Discuss safety aspects where appropriate, for example when boiling the pasta. Make sure the children know how important it is to ask for adult help when dealing with dangerous things like this. Make sure they know why boiling the pasta is dangerous. (Tell them that *boiling* means very, very hot and if the boiling water was spilt or splashed on their skin, it would burn and hurt them.)

PSHE and citizenship activities

◆ Ask a parent helper or classroom assistant to work with the children in groups to actually follow the recipe to make the house. Let each group show their version to the others and then let them eat their houses! Talk specifically about hygiene rules and how the food must be covered and not touched by everyone if we are to eat it. Introduce the term *germ* and explain how germs make us ill, for example colds. Tell the children that germs are carried on hands and in the air so we have to protect food from these by washing our hands and covering food.

◆ Ask the children to make a set of guidelines for the cookery area about keeping the area clean, tidy and free from germs, and rules for personal hygiene whilst preparing food. Display these in the cookery area.

◆ Take a group of children to a local shop to buy the ingredients, or make a class shop so they can cost out how much the recipe would be to make. Help the children to do this as the amounts may be difficult, but it is important that they realise how much food can cost. Link this discussion to poorer countries that have little food and explain what types of food children in these countries consume. Make sure the children realise that crisps and sweets are very much a privilege. Discuss how lucky they are that they have lots of food to eat and discuss who pays for this food.

◆ Discuss with the children why this recipe is healthy. Talk about other healthy options instead of pasta, such as potatoes, rice and bread. Why do we need this type of food at almost every meal? (This type of food fills us up and gives us lots of energy. It is called carbohydrate and is what helps us be able to run around, concentrate and so on.) Discuss with the children the idea of crop foods and how they can be made into foods that fill us up. Have a go at potato printing, breadmaking or making pictures with rice to reinforce these alternatives.

◆ Investigate different types of pastas and rice with the class. Make collections of different varieties and look at similarities and differences. Ask the children to make tables to show this information. They can write descriptions about each and some could investigate which parts of the world they come from and how they are grown. These can then be displayed.

Further literacy ideas

◆ Investigate the *i before e except after c* rule by looking for food words with *ie* and *ei* in them (*ingredients*, *sieve*). Extend this to all words (*receive*). Make a list of words to sort and display.

◆ The children can write their own instructions for making a food picture. This may be one they make in class, or perhaps they or their mums and dads make pictures with the food on their plates sometimes and the children could describe this.

◆ Investigate the types of language used in instructional text, for example *boil the…, mix the…, pour on…* Give the children sentences to rewrite in this way.

◆ Cut up the instructions for the recipe and make them into a jigsaw by asking the children to remake the text up in the right order. Then try with an unknown text – this will be much harder for them.

Genre
humorous
poetry

Hair

I despair
About hair
  With all the fuss
  For us
Of snipping
And clipping,
  Of curling
  And twirling,
Of tying
And drying,
  And lopping
  And flopping
And flurries
And worries,
  About strength,
  The length,
As it nears
The ears
  Or shoulder.
  When you're older
It turns grey
Or goes away
  Or leaves a fuzz
  Hair does!

by Max Fatchen

TEACHING WITH TEXT PSHE AND CITIZENSHIP ages 5–7   KEEPING HEALTHY
SCHOLASTIC

Hair

Display a selection of hair accessories: hairbrush, hairslides, shampoo bottles, and so on.

PSHE and citizenship learning objectives

◆ To recognise what likes and dislikes (1a).

◆ To be able to take part in a simple debate about topical issues (2b).

◆ To recognise choices can be made (2c).

◆ To be able to make simple choices that improve health and well-being (3a).

Vocabulary

Hair, hairbrush, shampoo, long, short, blonde, ginger, curly, straight.

Discussing the text

◆ Read the poem to the children with them following the reading. Ask what they think the poem is about and go through it again, discussing each pair of lines and what the poet is saying. As points arise, discuss with the children any experiences or feelings similar to these they may have.

◆ Once the children are familiar with the content and some of the more difficult words, read it through again with all the children trying to join in.

◆ Discuss with the children how they feel about their hair. Who has bad hair days sometimes? Is long hair more of a problem than short hair? Who has been to the hairdresser's or barber's and felt embarrassed about coming to school the next day?

◆ Focus on the last four lines and discuss with the children what this means. Talk about how hair changes as we get older, and how men can lose their hair as they become more elderly. Who do they know in their family who has grey or white hair, or who is balding?

PSHE and citizenship activities

◆ Discuss with the children why they think we have hair on our heads (it gives protection from the sun in summer and helps keep the heat in our bodies during the winter). Get them to think about the fact that when they get hot from running around it is always their head that is the hottest part of their body.

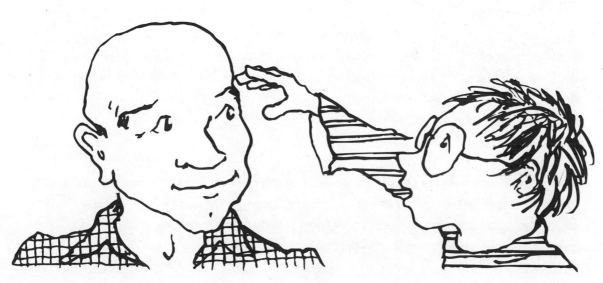

◆ Discuss the different types of hair there are (straight, wavy, curly, blonde, brown, ginger). Ask the children to write a description of their own hair. Look at the similarities and differences between a group of children in the class, being careful to be positive about everyone's hair. Make a graph to show similarities and differences in colour and texture. Display this with the children's descriptions of their own hair.

◆ Ask the children to talk about how they look after their hair daily and weekly. Discuss how we need to brush our hair to make it look neat and tidy, but also to keep it healthy by spreading out the oils produced by our hair follicles on our head. Discuss washing hair and why we do this. Many children will not like having their hair washed. Discuss why. The children can write about having their hair washed, when it happens, how it is done and how they feel about it. There will probably be differences here between those children with short and long hair.

◆ Encourage the children to provide arguments for simple discussion or debate about having short or long hair, stating the advantages and disadvantages of each.

◆ Get the children to write a set of instructions each about looking after hair. Make these into small booklets entitled *Hair care* and ask the children to illustrate them with appropriately labelled diagrams.

◆ Invite the local nurse into the classroom to inform the children of head lice, and how to avoid and get rid of them. You may like to ask parents to attend this session, perhaps holding it first thing or at the end of the day.

Further literacy ideas

◆ Look at words with an *air* rime, such as *lair, hair, fair*.

◆ Extend the investigation into words with *ai* in them, such as *rain* and *stain* to help the children identify the different phonemes *ai* makes. Sort the words from both activities into sound groups.

◆ Ask the children to find out more information about hair and how we should look after it by looking in information books or using a CD-ROM. They could also write to a local hairdresser for information.

◆ Design a class poster explaining how to look after hair.

◆ Explore the rhyming couplets in the poem with the children. Look at letter patterns and make similar collections of words, for example words ending in –*ing*, -*air* and –*ength* and so on.

◆ Ask the children to try to write their own poems using the format of the one in the text (rhyming couplets, short sharp lines and spaced out in a similar pattern).

◆ Look at antonyms linked to hair style and colour, such as *clean/dirty, blonde/black, curly/straight*.

Getting ready for bed

Genre
*non-fiction
procedural
text*

Introduction to the text
It's Amy's bedtime. She has written a list of things she needs to do before going to sleep, but they are not in the right order.

It's half-past seven, time for bed. What do I have to remember to do?

Get in the bath.

Take off my clothes.

Dry myself with a big, fluffy, warm towel.

Wash my face, behind my ears, around my mouth, under my chin.

Take off my shoes and socks.

Wash my body, legs and arms, between my toes, all the tricky bits I can't see.

Lather up the soap on my sponge.

Brush my teeth.

Have my supper and a nice milky drink.

Light out, 'night night'.

Sleep at last.

Put on my pyjamas.

Get into bed.

by Amy Makin

Getting ready for bed

Display the statements on individual cards so the children can use these to rearrange the order and complete the task.

PSHE and citizenship learning objectives

◆ To recognise likes and dislikes (1a).

◆ To recognise choices can be made (2c).

◆ To realise that people and other living things have needs (2e).

◆ To be able to make simple choices that improve their health and well-being (3a).

◆ To maintain personal hygiene (3b).

◆ To know the names of the main parts of the body (3e).

Vocabulary

First, last, bath, wash, lather, supper, parts of the body.

Discussing the text

◆ Look at the title and the first line with the children. Explain to them that the girl who wrote this has mixed up the order in which to get ready for bed, and that as a class they are going to try to help her sort out what she has to do. Read the list of actions with the children before having any discussion about the order. Ask them, in pairs, to decide which they would do first and last from this list and to report this back to the class – do they all have the same answers? (There will be differing ones, for example taking off socks and shoes may come before or after clothes, some children may go to sleep with the light on and an adult comes in and switches it off later.) Reinforce the fact that we all like to do things in different ways and discuss whether this matters (it does not).

◆ Debate with the children which lines they are going to use first and last in the class list of instructions. Stick these cards up on a board. Then continue working through the statements deciding whether each new one comes before or after the previous one until all the statements have been sorted. Read the final version to the children.

PSHE and citizenship activities

◆ Discuss with the children whether they get ready for bed in the same order as Amy. Get them to write their own list of pre-bedtime activities or to draw their own cartoon strip to show the order in which they get ready for bed.

◆ As a class, write a list of reminders for getting up and getting ready for school in the morning. Discuss with the children how their routines differ depending on personal preference.

◆ Talk with the children about why we need to have a wash, brush our teeth and change our clothes to go to bed. Talk about general hygiene and why we need to keep ourselves clean to keep healthy.

◆ What are the tricky bits Amy cannot see? (Under her arms, her bottom, between her toes.) Why do we need to be careful to wash these bits? Discuss general hygiene issues here. Talk about body functions and waste products. If we don't wash places where we sweat, we will become smelly.

◆ Discuss the activity of brushing teeth. How many children brush their teeth once a day, twice a day or more? Make a chart to show this information. Can the children who do it more than twice a day explain why? Can they present an argument to persuade others to do this too? What flavour toothpaste do the children use? Which is the favourite flavour in the class?

◆ Ask a dentist or dental nurse to visit and talk to the children about oral hygiene. Collect leaflets that tell children how to look after their teeth, or use a children's toothpaste or toothbrush packet with advice and instructions on them, and show these to the class. These also often have addresses to write to for additional information. In pairs, ask the children to write a set of instructions for brushing teeth and display these with other information about oral hygiene.

◆ Set up a dentist's play area. Use the collected leaflets and ask the children to make posters to encourage good oral hygiene.

Further literacy ideas

◆ Put the statements written by the class about getting ready for school onto individual cards so the children, in pairs, can have a go at re-ordering this text as well as the getting-ready-for-bed text.

◆ Investigate roots and suffixes linked to the tense change of verbs, such as *wash, washed, washing*; *brush, brushed, brushing*. Give the children a sentence and ask them to write it in three different ways, changing the tense each time.

◆ The children can write a narrative non-fiction version of either getting up or going to bed. Look at their likes and dislikes about this, such as how many times a parent nags(!), how inconvenient it is going to bed when it is light on a summer's night, how cosy they feel wrapped up in bed with a hot water bottle on a cold winter's night. Encourage the children to use lots of adjectives and adverbs to describe how they feel.

◆ The children can send for information using an address from a toothpaste or toothbrush packet, writing letters explaining why they want the information and for which age range of readers it is for. They can then use this information to make their own display about looking after teeth, or to present to another class, or in assembly.

Citizenship

Citizenship in its own right is a new concept to the infant classroom, yet when considering the PSHE and citizenship syllabus it is clear that many of the objectives are routinely being met in the daily work and life of the classroom and school. Though the context of section 2 of the non-statutory guidelines in the syllabus is a mixture of criteria, its main thrust is to introduce children to the notion of collective responsibility for others, animals and the environment. It also seeks to develop a sense of empowerment and democratic philosophy. The class and the school settings work well in this respect. These encourage adherence to a given set of rules, often established in discussion with the children, and upheld in order to create a better and safer social environment for them. This mimics society's laws and the legislative process.

Section 2 also introduces very important distinctions between right and wrong, and stresses the principle that a child can choose to do right or wrong, but must ultimately take responsibility for the consequences of that choice. Empathy is an emergent skill in this section of the syllabus too. At Key Stage 2 this section develops to include discussions on bullying. For this reason this anti-social behaviour (required in section 4 of the syllabus) will be included in this book.

Most of the literacy segments, discussion and activities in this chapter will deal with seeing things from different points of view, doing right and wrong, and looking after animals and the environment. There are cross-curricular links here with geography and RE.

The Three Pigs

Introduction to the text

This story is about three pigs who decide that they hate living in the overcrowded, noisy city in a high-rise flat. They move to the country but forget that the big bad wolf lives there and eats pigs. Each pig builds its own house, but the first two build theirs badly and end up as the wolf's dinner. The third pig is more intelligent than his friends. He builds his house out of bricks and mortar. The wolf first tries blowing the house down with his *I'll huff and I'll puff and I'll blow your house down*, but all that happens is that he exhausts himself. Next, he pretends to be the pig's friend and tries, several times, to lure the pig outside. The pig is too clever for the wolf and chases him away. Eventually, the wolf loses his temper…

The wolf was furious, and he dropped all pretence at being the pig's friend. Snarling and spluttering, he clawed his way onto the roof and started to wriggle down the chimney.

Pig popped his largest pan onto the fire. It was full of boiling water and spring greens. With a snarl and a clatter, the wolf fell into the pot, and Pig slammed down the lid. Two hours later, he gobbled the wolf up, with asparagus tips and potato croquettes.

With the wolf gone, it was quite safe to live in the country. More and more people moved from the tower blocks and built houses around Pig's house. Strong, brick houses.

Pig looked at the cramped and noisy streets.

"I wish I was back on the 39th floor," he thought.

by Tony Ross

The Three Pigs

Display a scene of the clever pig looking miserable outside his green brick house in a crowded street, with a speech bubble saying *I should have stayed in the city*.

PSHE and citizenship learning objectives

◆ To recognise what is fair and unfair, and what is right and wrong (1a).

◆ To think about ourselves and learn from experiences (1d).

◆ To take part in a simple debate about topical issues (2b).

◆ To recognise choices can be made (2c).

◆ To recognise what harms the environment (2g).

◆ To know when to get people to help us (3g).

◆ To recognise how behaviour affects other people (4a).

◆ To take part in discussions (5c).

◆ To consider social and moral dilemmas in everyday life (5g).

◆ To be able to ask for help (5h).

Background notes

This clever adaptation of the traditional tale of *The Three Little Pigs* adds an environmental twist and much wry humour. The full story is well worth using in a Year 2 classroom.

Vocabulary

Wolf, huff and puff, right, wrong, countryside, city.

Discussing the text

◆ Read the first part of the introduction to the text to the children, up to the pigs deciding to build their own houses. Ask the children to explain why the pigs wanted to move to the country. Do they agree with that view? Why? List on one side of a flip chart the reasons they give for not liking the city. Then list on the other side the attractions of the countryside, after asking the children what the pigs were hoping it would be like there.

◆ Ask the children why they think that the other two pigs ended up being eaten by the wolf. (The children may recall the traditional tale about the houses of straw and wood.) Why didn't the pigs build their houses of brick? Allow all reasonable suggestions as the story and fable don't say (they weren't clever enough, didn't know about the danger from the wolf, it was quicker or easier to build, and so on).

◆ Ask the children for ideas about the kind of trickery the wolf got up to in the story. Give time for them to discuss some ideas with a partner then get them to feed those ideas back to the class.

◆ Re-read the text up to the eating of the wolf. Ask the children why the wolf got so angry. Introduce the term *thwarted*. Have the children ever been angry when they couldn't get their own way, for example about being first in the line, or having the use of the felts first, or wanting to speak to the teacher? Ask the children what they thought the wolf should have done (gone away and given up). Why?

◆ Ask the children whether they think it was right for the pig to kill and eat the wolf. Allow free discussion of the moral problem. The wolf would have killed and eaten the pig, but whilst it was right for the pig to protect himself, was it necessary to kill the wolf? Was it right to eat the wolf? Explore the ideas given by the children. If workable, bring out the idea that *two wrongs don't make a right*. The compromise solution would have been to send the wolf into exile, or negotiate a peace treaty – explain that this is an agreement to *live and let live*.

◆ Focus on the final section with the children. Make the point that as a result of killing the wolf, others flocked into the, now safe, countryside. Did the pig end up happy ever after? Why not?

P SHE and citizenship activities

◆ Discuss the problems of living in a crowded city or town with the class. What are the negative aspects about it? (Litter, dirt, crowds, noise, lack of green spaces and places to play, car fumes.) Can the children suggest how we could make things better in the city or town? What do they think are the negative aspects about living in the countryside? (Friends a long way away, no cinemas, theatres or fast-food restaurants, too quiet!)

◆ In pairs, get one child to write a letter to a friend who lives in the country explaining how miserable it is in the city. The other child can write at the same time to say how much he or she wants to come and live in the city. Get them to exchange letters and read each other's, then role-play a telephone conversation between the friends to describe life in the city and the countryside.

◆ Discuss the situation in the text where the pig has succeeded in thwarting the wolf and the wolf is getting really angry. Who could help the wolf and the pig sort this problem out? In threes, get the children to role-play a scene where the wolf has failed to blow down the last pig's house, one child taking on the part of the wolf, another the pig and a third a police officer. The police officer has to try and succeed in getting the wolf and the pig to agree to a peaceful compromise. After the role-play the children can write a sequel to the situation they acted out. What happened after the compromise was reached?

◆ The children can draw a storyboard of a time when they got angry and frustrated because they couldn't have their way. Encourage them to add key sentences or speech bubbles to their pictures. What happened in the story in the end? Who could have helped them solve their problems?

Further literacy ideas

◆ Look at the traditional phrase *I'll huff and I'll puff and I'll blow your house down*. As a class, compile the past-tense version. (*And he huffed and he puffed and he blew the house down.*)

◆ Remind the children how the wolf was expressing himself as he went down Pig's chimney. Ask the children to come up with some similar types of verbs to describe the different ways we can speak (*whispered, gargled, choked, gasped, stuttered, hissed, squeaked, spat*).

◆ The children can make a wordsearch with the verbs that were suggested, then write sentences using their three favourite verbs.

◆ Look at examples of proverbs such as *Live and let live, Two wrongs don't make a right*. Ask the children to write a proverb with an illustration of the point made.

◆ Look at *uff* and *ff* words with the children. Try to find new words to add to a wordbank (such as *muff, cuff, shuffle, muffle, duffle coat, cliff, waffle*).

◆ Ask the children to imagine the wolf has tried to trick the pig and failed, but instead of trying to climb down the chimney he uses his mobile phone to speak to his mother. Get them to write a play about that telephone conversation. What does the wolf say to his mum? What does she advise him to do? This could also be done on the computer as an e-mail correspondence.

◆ Try to contact another school in an opposing location to yours (urban or rural) by researching websites for schools. The children can communicate with their opposite parts via e-mail.

The Three Little Wolves and the Big Bad Pig

Genre
reworking of a familiar tale

Introduction to the text

This is a story that might seem familiar to you. It is about three young wolves that are sent out into the world to live happily. They build a house but it is attacked by a big bad pig who huffs and puffs and blows their house down. The wolves escape, but then decide to build a house out of concrete. The pig attacks it with drills and destroys the house. They next build a house like a fortress with wire fences and alarms and reinforced steel walls. The pig, laughing all the while, blows it up with dynamite and the little wolves only just escape. The wolves don't know what to do to protect themselves.

"Something must be wrong with our building materials," they said. "We have to try something different. But *what?*"

At that moment, they saw a flamingo bird coming along pushing a wheelbarrow full of flowers.

"Please, will you give us some flowers?" asked the little wolves.

"With pleasure," said the flamingo bird and gave them lots of flowers. So the three little wolves built themselves a house of flowers.

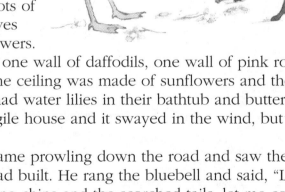

One wall was of marigolds, one wall of daffodils, one wall of pink roses and one wall of cherry blossom. The ceiling was made of sunflowers and the floor was a carpet of daisies. They had water lilies in their bathtub and buttercups in their fridge. It was a rather fragile house and it swayed in the wind, but it was very beautiful.

Next day, the big bad pig came prowling down the road and saw the house of flowers that the little wolves had built. He rang the bluebell and said, "Little frightened wolves with trembling chins and the scorched tails, let me come in!"

"No, no, no," said the three little wolves. "By the hair on our chinny-chin-chins, we will not let you in, not for all the tea leaves in our china teapot!"

"Then I'll huff and I'll puff and I'll blow your house down!" said the pig.

But as he took a deep breath, ready to huff and puff, he smelled the soft scent of the flowers. It was fantastic. And because the scent took his breath away, the pig took another breath and then another. Instead of huffing and puffing, he began to sniff.

He sniffed deeper and deeper until he was quite filled with the fragrant scent. His heart became tender and he realised how horrible he had been in the past. In other words, he became a big *good* pig. He started to sing and to dance the tarantella.

by Eugene Trivizas

illustrated by Helen Oxenbury

The Three Little Wolves and the Big Bad Pig

Display a scene of the big pig and the wolves playing together beside the house of flowers.

PSHE and citizenship learning objectives

◆ To recognise likes and dislikes (1a).

◆ To think about ourselves and learn from experiences (1d).

◆ To recognise choices can be made, and the difference between right and wrong (2c).

◆ To recognise how behaviour affects other people (4a).

◆ To know that there are different forms of bullying and that bullying is wrong, and how to get help to deal with bullying (4e).

Background notes

This is a very skilled reworking of the traditional tale of the wolf and the three pigs, only in this story the victims are three little wolves and the enemy is a big bad pig. The story is one that works very well in full, but this extract focuses on the idea of non-violent conflict resolution, where meeting force with force fails. It has a clever twist that should amuse children. This text works best if children are already familiar with the traditional story of the three little pigs and could be used together with the previous text.

Vocabulary

Destroy, nasty, big, bad, bullying, good, peace.

Discussing the text

◆ Read the introduction to the text and ask the children if they recognise the parallel with the traditional version of the tale (they may already have looked at the text on page 123). Then discuss the basic differences between the two stories.

◆ Ask the children to predict what is going to happen in the text. What can the wolves do now if nothing they build, no security device, seems to keep out the big bad pig? What would they do? (Ask the police to protect them? Pay for a security firm to protect their house?) The children might answer with threatened violence, suggesting using guns or weapons. If this happens, allow the suggestion but then counter-suggest that the pig would probably have a big gun too. The wolves could get killed.

◆ Read the text extract to the class up to the pig's threat to huff and puff until the flower house has blown down. Ask the children why the wolves would have chosen flowers for their building materials. What will happen next?

◆ Read to the end of the text. Clarify with the children that they understand what happened in the end. (The flowers made the big bad pig feel better.) Ask the children what will happen next. Do they think the pig and the wolves will start to play together and become very good friends, or will the pig have another grumpy or nasty mood and be horrible again? (Allow a range of responses, though the story actually concludes with them all being friends, so develop the ideas of a peaceful outcome.)

◆ Ask the children which version of the story they preferred and why.

◆ Discuss with the children the possible reasons why the pig was bad. List the ideas on a flip chart. In view of the ending, do they think the pig was bad through and through, or just grumpy and miserable? Would he have a better time blowing things up or playing with his friends?

PSHE and citizenship activities

◆ Ask the children to retell the story from the point of view of the big bad pig, and to first think about the way the pig was feeling and why he was so nasty. Get them to draw two pictures of the pig, one with a speech bubble with him cross and nasty, the other with him skipping about the fields, happy and content.

◆ Discuss with the children whether they think the pig was being a bully when he was being so nasty. How does a bully behave? (He or she deliberately does things to frighten or hurt other people. He or she enjoys hurting people and making them scared.) How can the children stop someone bullying them, or bullying someone else? (Tell them to stop. Seek adult help if they will not stop.)

◆ Talk to the children about times when they have been grumpy or cross. What made them feel better? Ask them to make a list of things they can do to make themselves feel better when they are miserable or grumpy.

◆ Get the children to role-play different ways of stopping themselves staying cross. How could they help a friend who was feeling cross and miserable? Get them to act that out too.

Further literacy ideas

◆ Summarise on the flip chart the children's suggestions for the characteristics of the plot and characters in both stories, the traditional one and this version. Highlight the similarities and the differences.

◆ In pairs, ask the children to come up with a new chapter to end the story – what happened after the pig felt better?

◆ Ask the children to write a review on the word processor summarising the story and what they like and dislike about it. This can be printed out and illustrated.

◆ Work on extending the children's vocabulary for describing feelings when in a bad or a good mood. Get them to act out these words in groups.

The Teddy Robber

Genre
*fantasy with
a familiar
setting*

Introduction to the text

This is a story about a little boy called Tom whose Teddy is stolen one night by a big giant. Tom follows the giant to his huge castle and watches as the Giant puts Tom's Teddy in an enormous cupboard already filled to the top with teddies. Tom discovers that the Giant is the Teddy Robber because he has lost his own Teddy. So Tom offers to help the Giant look for it.

"We'll never find it," said the Giant, and they sat down and had a mug of cocoa together.

"Would you like a biscuit?" asked the Giant politely.

"The biscuits are on your pillow," said Tom.

The Giant looked surprised. "They ought to be on the shelf – the pillow is where my Teddy used to be." And he began to cry all over again.

"If the biscuits are on your pillow," said Tom, "then perhaps your Teddy is… on the shelf!"

"My Teddy! My Teddy! You've found him! How can I ever thank you?"

"First you can give me back *my* Teddy. And then you must put back all those stolen Teddies – straight away!" said Tom.

by Ian Beck

The Teddy Robber

Display a scene from the Giant's castle when Tom first speaks to him and the Giant confesses that he is a Teddy Robber. All the children can contribute a painting of their favourite teddy for the display. Speech bubbles can record the salient points of the text.

Also create a 3-D display of all sorts of teddies.

PSHE and citizenship learning objectives

◆ To recognise what is fair and unfair, and what is right and wrong (1a).

◆ To recognise choices can be made (2c).

◆ To agree and follow the rules for their group and classroom, and understand how rules help them (2d).

◆ To contribute to the life of the class and school (2h).

◆ To recognise how behaviour affects other people (4a).

◆ To take and share responsibility (5a).

◆ To make real choices about behaviour (5d).

◆ To develop relationships through work and play (5f).

◆ To consider social and moral dilemmas in everyday life (5g).

◆ To be able to ask for help (5h).

Vocabulary

Steal, stolen, right, wrong, understand, forgive, make amends.

Discussing the text

◆ Read the introduction to the text with the class. Ask the children if they think this is a real story, or a make-believe one. How do they know? (The presence of a giant.) Discuss with the children why the Giant might have stolen the teddy. (He was horrible and wanted to upset children, he simply wanted to, he liked teddies.) Do they think all the other teddies in the cupboard were stolen?

◆ What do the children think the Giant has done wrong? (Taken Tom's and other teddies without asking – point out he has stolen the teddies.) How do they think Tom felt about having his teddy stolen? Record these feeling words on a flip chart.

◆ Ask the children why they think Tom agreed to help the Giant find his own teddy. Do they think Tom might have felt angry at first? Why was he not angry anymore? (He realised why the Giant had stolen all the teddies.) Introduce the terms forgive and understand.

◆ Ask the children if there has been a time when they've been hurt or upset by someone, but then they've understood and forgiven the person, for example a younger brother or sister taking their toys.

◆ What do the children think the Giant should have done instead of stealing other children's teddies? (Got someone to help him find his own Teddy, or bought a new one.) What should they do if they want to play with someone else's toys? (Ask if they can borrow or share them.)

◆ Read the part of the text where the Giant's teddy is found. Ask the children what Tom's attitude towards the Giant is once his teddy is found. (He tells him off and insists that he make amends.) Put the term make amends on the flip chart and help the children understand what it means. Ask them what the Giant has to do to make amends.

◆ Ask the children if the Giant has learned his lesson. Will he steal again? Allow the children to express their own views on this.

PSHE and citizenship activities

◆ Bring in your own teddy and show it to the children. Discuss with them what is so special about teddies. Ask them to paint a picture of their favourite teddy or soft toy and write about why they like it so much. If any of the children don't have a teddy, they can draw and name your teddy and say what they like about it.

◆ Ask the children to pretend individually that they are one of the children in the story who wakes up with their teddy missing. How do they feel and what do they do? On a sheet of paper divided vertically down the middle get them to draw a picture on the left-hand side of themselves without their teddy, surrounded with words that describe how they feel. On the right-hand side of the page they can draw another picture of themselves waking up and finding their teddy under the bed. They can record the feeling words in this situation too.

◆ Discuss with the children possible alternative versions of the story. What should the Giant have done once he found that his teddy was missing? (Asked his mum or dad for help, or asked Tom to help him.) How would the story end if he had done this? Get the children to role-play different versions in groups of two or three.

◆ Formally re-enact the story in play form for an assembly, with the moral points explained and advice given about how the Giant should have behaved. Replay the story in assembly with an alternative ending, for example where the Giant asks Tom to help him find his teddy, Tom finds it, both are happy and Tom befriends the Giant. Alternatively, the Giant could ask his mum or dad to help him find the teddy.

◆ Discuss with the children times when they have done something very silly or wrong. They may have been upset or frustrated, and shouted or hit out at a friend who wasn't nice or wouldn't let them be the leader in a game. Ask the children, in pairs, to tell their own stories to each other and work out how they could have solved the problem without doing anything wrong.

◆ Look at the class rules and see if the children can identify the one that tells them not to take things from other people. Ask what sort of things might be taken in the class that shouldn't be (pencils, rubbers, felts). Ask the children what they should do if they haven't got something they need (ask to borrow it).

Further literacy ideas

◆ As a class, compare the traditional story of Jack and the Beanstalk with this Giant story. Look at the characters of the two giants. What are the differences?

◆ Plan a whole-class teddy bears' picnic. The children can write invitations to their teddies, plan a menu, help prepare the food, hold the picnic and tidy away afterwards.

◆ Ask the children to write a letter as another child's teddy to say thank you for the picnic.

◆ Take photographs of the picnic (this could be with a digital camera) that the children can use to illustrate a class newspaper report of the event.

◆ Investigate words with the children that take *dy* endings, such as *teddy, ready, handy*. Make a collection to display.

Citizen rap

Genre
modern rhyming poem/song

Introduction to the text
This text should be read in a rap-type rhythm.

Citizen citizen, be a super citizen,
Citizen, citizen, be a super citizen.

Don't drop litter in the street
Keep town centres sweet and neat,
Don't cut flowers in the park
Nor on the walls, do make your mark,
Play on swings the proper way
And fun you'll have, all through the day,
Clean and tidy, we will be
In street and park, for all to see.

Citizen, citizen, be a super citizen,
Citizen, citizen, be a super citizen.

In the country, fresh air pursue
But take your rubbish home with you,
Keep the noise down near and far
And never leave a gate ajar,
Don't trample crops or scare the beasts
Just sit, enjoy your picnic feast,
Keep to paths and tracks and ways
To make the most of your holidays.

Citizen, citizen, you're a super citizen,
Citizen, citizen, we are super citizens.

by Gillian Goddard

Citizen rap

Display two scenes, one of a town and one of the country, with the countryside and urban codes written and placed in the middle.

PSHE and citizenship learning objectives

◆ To recognise what is right and wrong (1a).

◆ To know how to set simple goals (1e).

◆ To be able to take part in a simple debate about topical issues (2b).

◆ To recognise choices can be made (2c).

◆ To agree and follow rules and understand how rules help (2d).

◆ To realise that people and other living things have needs, and that there are responsibilities to meet them (2e).

◆ To know what improves and harms the local, natural and built environments (2g).

◆ To contribute to the life of the class and school (2h).

◆ To recognise how behaviour affects other people (4a).

◆ To feel positive about ourselves (5b).

◆ To be able to consider social and moral dilemmas in everyday life (5g).

Vocabulary

Citizen, countryside code, litter, graffiti.

Discussing the text

◆ Read the text to the children, focusing on correctly phrasing and delivering it in a rap style. Ask the children what a rap is. How can they tell if this is a rap? (A strong rhythmic beat with short, jabbing phrases that rhyme.)

◆ Rehearse the rap with the children.

◆ Look with the children at the rhyming couplets of the rap poem. Ask them to suggest alternative rhyming words to the last word on each line, for example *street/meat*, *park/dark*.

◆ What do the children think the rap song is all about? Talk about what a citizen is. How do citizens behave? What do they do? (Obey laws and look after their community and location.)

◆ Focus on the first verse. Ask the children what it is telling them (how best to behave in the town). What does the poem mean by *Nor on the walls, do make your mark*? Put up the word *graffiti* on a flip chart. Explain why it is wrong to do this.

◆ Look at the second verse with the children. Is that set in the countryside or town? What is it telling them to do and not to do?

PSHE and citizenship activities

◆ Look at some of the things the song says we shouldn't do. Ask the children why we mustn't do these things. Establish that there are very good reasons for not dropping litter, or walking across farmers' fields. Record these as *Things we must not do* in one column on a flip chart and *Reasons why* in another.

◆ Put the word *citizen* on the flip chart. Ask the children to suggest ways they themselves can be good citizens, for example putting litter in the bin, obeying the school rules and the rules in the park, looking out for one another and keeping safe, not being a nuisance and not annoying people.

◆ Ask the children to write a series of rules for the classroom or playground based on one verse of the rap song. Get them to word-process and print these out on the computer.

◆ Look at the countryside code. Ask the children to draw illustrations to go with the rules suggested.

◆ Walk to the park with the class and look for signs that state what we can and cannot do, for example *Don't walk on the grass*, *Keep dogs off the grass*, *Don't pick the flowers* or age limits for play apparatus. Also note where there is any litter and the location of the litter bins. If appropriate, take black sacks and rubber gloves and ask volunteers to help pick up the paper litter and clear the park up. (Do not allow the children to pick up anything sharp.)

◆ Walk around the school with the children and note where there is litter. Investigate with the children where the bins are and discuss if they are most effectively used, and if not, why not? Ask for suggested improvements that could be made and write as a class to the headteacher or governors suggesting these changes and explaining why they are necessary.

◆ Ask a park keeper, local government officer or police liaison officer to come and talk to the children about being a good citizen.

◆ Ask the children to write a newspaper story about a group of children who decided to make their local area look better and received an award as a result. Encourage the children to draw a picture to accompany their article.

◆ The class could perform the rap with appropriate gestures to the rest of the school as part of a good citizen assembly.

Further literacy ideas

◆ The children can work on a similar rap for cleaning their teeth or keeping clean.

◆ Cut and mix up the verse lines and ask the children to reorder the poem by matching the rhyming words. As a handwriting practice they can each copy two lines. These can then be displayed as a collective poem.

◆ Look together at words with the rime *ap*, for example *rap*, *tap*, *snap*, *clap*. Use them to make up a rhyme with actions and sound effects. This can be supported with instruments that make the sound effects, such as a tambourine and whistle.

◆ Investigate the phoneme *z*. Get the children to use dictionaries to find words beginning with *z*. Can they find any other words including a *z* in their reading books?

◆ Using the phrase *super citizen*, how many other words can the children make from it?

Mine!

Genre
fiction with a familiar setting

Isabel went to play with Claudia.
She climbed onto Claudia's rocking horse.
"Mine!" shrieked Claudia and pushed her off.
Isabel picked up Claudia's Carrot Top doll.
"Mine!" screamed Claudia and snatched it away.

by Hiawyn Oram
illustrated by Mary Rees

Mine!

Display a large-scale version of the rule about sharing with friends.

PSHE and learning objectives

◆ To recognise likes and dislikes, what is fair and unfair, and what is right and wrong (1a).

◆ To think about ourselves and learn from experiences (1d).

◆ To recognise choices can be made (2c).

◆ To be able to agree and follow rules (2d).

◆ To realise that people have needs and that there are responsibilities to meet them (2e).

◆ To recognise how behaviour affects other people (4a).

◆ To know that friends should care for each other (4d).

Background notes

This text deals with a very powerful set of emotions surrounding the possession of things and the need to temper these emotions by sharing with friends. The full story is well worth reading to the children because it has a dry, humorous conclusion. This extract, however, focuses on the problems identified.

Vocabulary

Mine, selfish, share.

Discussing the text

◆ Read the extract with the children. Ask the children who Isabel is (Claudia's friend). Ask what Claudia is like. How old do they think she is? How can they tell? Ask if they have any younger brothers or sisters who behave like Claudia.

◆ Discuss Claudia's selfish behaviour with the children. Do they know what the word *selfish* means? Why is it wrong to be so selfish? Can they come up with other examples of selfish behaviour?

◆ Ask the children what they would want to say to Claudia if they were Isabel? Would they want to be her friend? If not, why not? Make the point that if we are not prepared to share our things with friends, they won't be friends for very long.

◆ Look at the text together and spot the use of exclamation marks. What does this mark tell the children about the meaning of the text and how to say the words? Get a confident child to read the speech parts with expression as a playlet.

◆ Ask the children what they think will happen next in the story. Offer some possibilities to help them, for example would Isabel stop being friends with Claudia, would they have a fight, would an adult intervene? Record their ideas on a flip chart. Then, as a class, choose one ending and ask the children to collectively suggest some dialogue, recording this on the flip chart.

PSHE and citizenship activities

◆ Ask the children to imagine that they are Claudia's mother. What advice would they give to their daughter? Get them to act out in pairs a scenario where advice is given, one child taking the part of Claudia and the other the mother.

◆ Ask the class to come up with a rule about playing together based upon Claudia's bad behaviour. The rule should use the word *share*.

◆ The children can write a story about a selfish friend who won't share things. Ask them to include how they manage to get their friend to change their ways and share things.

◆ Get the children to practise sharing things in the classroom, for example their pencils and rulers.

◆ Ask the children what they should do if someone lends or shares their toys or pencils with them. (They should play with or use them carefully so as not to damage or lose them. They should also return them to their friend and be prepared to share their own things.) Make up a sharing contract for the class collectively or allow the children to do this in pairs, stating for example *I will share my things with you. You will use them with care, return them to me and let me share your things*.

Further literacy ideas

◆ Ask the children to draw a storyboard of the text, with the key word *Mine!* featured in it.

◆ Look with the children for matching sets of words, *mine/yours*, *his/hers*, *he/she*, *ours/theirs* and display these.

◆ The children can practise writing an exclamation mark in different sizes and with different pens and pencils.

◆ Get the children to write a typical sentence that could have an exclamation mark at the end.

◆ Investigate the vowel–consonant–vowel rule (the magic e) with the class using the word *mine*. Find other words that use this rule, for example *cap/cape*, *hat/hate*.

I want a pet!

Genre
play

List of characters

Mum

Dad

Jenny, aged 7

Ken, aged 3

Act 1: the kitchen

MUM: What do you want for your birthday Jenny?

JENNY: I want a pet.

DAD: No!

JENNY: But that's not fair! Why can't I have a pet?

DAD: Because they are smelly, expensive and troublesome things.

KEN: I want a pet. I want a pet. I want a pet.

MUM: Eat your wheatiflakes Ken.

JENNY: Couldn't I just have a little pet?

MUM: Perhaps we could have something small, Daddy?

Dad growls.

MUM: What sort of pet were you thinking of Jenny?

JENNY: A big fluffy dog.

DAD: No!

JENNY: Why not Dad?

DAD: The house is too small.

MUM: It would leave hair and mess everywhere.

DAD: It would dig up the garden and would need to be taken out for walks every day, even in the rain.

KEN: I want a dog.

JENNY: Can I have a cat then?

DAD: No!

JENNY: Why not?

DAD: They make me sneeze.

MUM: They leave fur everywhere.

DAD: They make messes in the garden.

KEN: I want a cat.

JENNY: A goldfish?

Mum and Dad look at each other.

MUM: A pet is a commitment, dear.

KEN: I want a commitment.

DAD: You'd have to feed it each day and clean it out each week.

JENNY: I will, I promise.

KEN: I want a commitment.

DAD, MUM and JENNY: Eat your wheatiflakes Ken.

Act 2: four weeks later

JENNY: It's your turn to feed the fish Ken.

KEN: I don't want to.

JENNY: It's your turn.

KEN: I don't want to.

JENNY: Nor do I.

Ken runs out to play with his friends. Jenny sighs.

MUM: You must clean the fish tank out Jenny. It smells.

JENNY: It's not fair. I always do it.

MUM: It's your fish Jenny.

JENNY: Can't you do it Mum? I want to play with my friends.

MUM: A pet is a commitment Jenny. It is a living thing not a toy. Clean out the fish.

Jenny growls and thinks I wish I didn't have a pet now.

by Gillian Goddard

I want a pet!

Display books about different sorts of pets. Also a goldfish bowl and goldfish.

PSHE and citizenship learning objectives

◆ To recognise what is right and wrong (1a).

◆ To know how to set simple goals (1e).

◆ To recognise choices can be made (2c).

◆ To realise that people and other living things have needs, and that there are responsibilities to meet them (2e).

◆ To recognise how behaviour affects other people and living things (4a).

◆ To take and share responsibility (5a).

Vocabulary

Pets, commitment, looking after.

Discussing the text

◆ Introduce the text to the class by explaining the play format and how it is read as dialogue. Read the first act of the text to the children and then repeat it using four children to play the parts. Ask the children if they have pets and what sort of pets they have. List these on a flip chart. Why do they want to have pets at home? (Something to look after, to play with, to talk to, to cuddle.)

◆ Discuss with the children the importance of choosing the right sort of pet for the home. Go through the examples in the play and ask why some of the pets weren't suitable for this family. What other pets would be wrong for this family and why? Would any other pets be suitable? (Hamster, budgie.)

◆ Discuss with the children what is meant by the word *commitment*. What was Mum warning Jenny about?

◆ Read the second act and then use three children to take the parts. How do Jenny and Ken feel about their pet now? Ask the children if they have pets they have to look after. What do they have to do for their pets to keep them happy and healthy? Is it a nuisance sometimes to have to look after them?

◆ Summarise the points raised so far about pets in a series of written instructions on the flip chart. For example, *1: Choose a pet with care. 2: Make sure you know how much looking after it will need. 3: Make sure you are willing to look after a pet.*

PSHE and citizenship activities

◆ In pairs, get the children to look at different types of pets, such as goldfish, cats, dogs, guinea pigs, rabbits, birds, rats, hamsters. Ask them to research what care their pet would need and what type of home, and to present a list to the rest of the class.

◆ Discuss with the children the benefits of having pets. Why do they like them? What is nice about having a pet? Discuss looking after wildlife in the garden as an extension to having an indoor pet, for example feeding the birds.

◆ Talk to the children about why it is important not to hurt pets and why they need lots of special care. The children can draw a picture of their favourite type of pet with the things the pet needs, such as food and drink, walks, straw, a basket.

◆ Bring in a small pet that is domesticated for the children to look at and/or handle. Make sure that children with allergies are protected. Ask the children in groups to make a model of the animal and make the things that the animal needs, for example a cat basket, a ball to play with, bowls of food and water, a brush, a litter basket.

◆ Give the children a set of six pictures of different pets and six items belonging to them. The children should match the right object to the right pet, for example *dog – lead, rabbit – lettuce.*

◆ Discuss with the children the different kinds of food different pets need.

◆ Get the children to write a story from a pet's point of view, describing its owner and how the owner looks after it.

◆ Bring in a goldfish and get the children to take turns feeding the fish and cleaning it out.

◆ Ask a vet or an RSPCA officer to come in and answer questions about pets, and to tell the children how to care for pets.

◆ Take the class to an RSPCA rescue centre to find out about the work done there and to teach the children how to look after pets.

Further literacy ideas

◆ Make a pet wordsearch for the children to work on.

◆ Compose some riddles and ask the children to guess the pet, for example *I am soft and furry, I have four legs, I catch mice, I make the sound miaow.* The children can then type in their own riddles on the computer, print them out and ask other children to guess the pet.

◆ Ask the class to find words that end in *et*, for example *pet, met, let, set, get, net, bet.* Use them to form a class wordbank.

◆ Look at the digraph *sh*, as in *fish*, with the children, and make a collection of similar words.

◆ In pairs, ask the children to write a simple dialogue about looking after a pet using the play format given in the text.

Infant School Disaster

Genre
*humorous
poem*

Peter pushed past Pauline
and Pauline pushed past Paul
so Peter pushed Paul sideways
then Pauline pushed them all…
Peter knocked the fire bell
and Pauline gave a shout
the dinner ladies heard them
and they all came running out!
They overturned their custard
and they slipped upon their sprouts
and upset all their puddings
and they upset all their stew…
The shepherds pie went flying
the pig bins went as well…
…then Pauline pushed past Peter
    and tried to stop the bell.
The teachers all came running
they met a sea of stew
and slipped in all the jelly
(the way that people do)
The teachers all went sprawling
in custard chips and peas
– jelly on their jackets
– and gravy on their knees.

by Peter Dixon

Infant school Disaster

Display two scenes of the dining room, one of chaos and one of order. In the middle write a list of rules for behaving well in the dining room.

PSHE and citizenship learning objectives

◆ To recognise what is right and wrong (1a).
◆ To recognise choices can be made (2c).
◆ To agree rules and follow them (2d).
◆ To recognise how behaviour affects other people (4a).

Vocabulary

Pushing, wrong, right, behaviour, rules, dinner ladies, fire alarm.

Discussing the text

◆ Read the poem through to the children, and then re-read with the children the first four lines. Ask the class what the children in the text are doing wrong. (Pushing in the dinner queue.) Why is pushing wrong? (It isn't fair, someone could get hurt, or damage could be done.)

◆ Read the next four lines with the class. What has happened? (The fire bell has sounded because Peter has fallen against it.) Was it an accident or do the children think Peter deliberately knocked the alarm? (Allow a range of views, but also focus closely on the text as it implies it was an accident.) Discuss with the children why we have fire alarms and what they should do in class and at dinner if the bell sounds. Remind the children that it is very wrong to ring the bell if there isn't a fire.

◆ Ask the class why the dinner helpers came out. What is their job and how should the children behave towards them? (They look after the children at dinnertime. The children should treat them with respect and do as they say.)

◆ Read the next eight lines (up to *and tried to stop the bell*). Ask the children what words describe what is happening here. Try to get the word *chaos* from the children or give it yourself, and put it on the flip chart. Ask why chaos in the dining room is not a good thing. (They could have accidents and get their clothes messy; people could get hurt; it would be impossible for them to eat their dinner.) Explain that this is why there are rules concerning the way they line up and move about the dining room. Ask the children to give you the rules for the dining room. List them on the flip chart. If there are no explicit rules, the class could design these.

◆ Finish reading the poem. What do the children think the teachers would do and say? In pairs, ask them to work out an answer and then feed it back to the whole class.

◆ Finally, discuss with the class what would have to happen next in the dining room. Who would clear up? What should happen to Peter, Pauline and Paul? Should they help clean up the mess?

PSHE and citizenship activities

◆ In small groups, take the children to find the location of the fire alarms. Discuss how and when they should be sounded.

◆ Make class posters telling other children in the school when a fire alarm should be sounded.

◆ Get the children to write cards to the dinner ladies (or midday assistants) to say thank you for looking after them during dinnertime.

◆ In groups, get the children to create their own rules for the dining room. Each group can present their rules to the whole class and then ask the children to vote on the best four rules. Once decided these rules can be word-processed, enlarged and printed off. A copy can be placed in the dining room.

◆ Ask the children to write a poem called 'Don't push!'. Each should start by describing what can happen if they push.

◆ Get the children to write a story about a time when some children misbehaved in the dining room. What happened? How did it end?

Further literacy ideas

◆ As a class, find as many words as you can that end with the digraph *sh*, for example *push, mash, bush, dish*. Add them to the class wordbank.

◆ Look together at the poem and identify the words at the end of each line that rhyme. Match these up in pairs, for example *Paul/all, shout/out*.

◆ Ask the children to look at the poem and find some action verbs that end in *-ing*, such as *running, sprawling, flying*. Ask them to find other *-ing* words that describe movement, such as *walking, pushing, dawdling, skipping, gliding*.

◆ Look in the class poetry anthologies and find other poems about naughty children. Read your favourite to the class. See if you can find other poems by Peter Dixon too.

◆ Look at the way the poem is written with the children. Ask how they know it is a poem (not writing to the right-hand side of the page but starting again with the next phrase, rhyming couplets). What other punctuation is used in this poem? (Exclamation marks, dashes, full stops, brackets and ellipses.)

◆ Ask the children to write a concluding stanza about what happened next in the same style of the poet.